120 NEEDLEPOINT DESIGN PROJECTS

120 NEEDLEPOINT DESIGN PROJECTS

Charles Barnes
David Blake

in collaboration with William Baker

CROWN PUBLISHERS, INC., NEW YORK

Our grateful acknowledgment to William Baker for his invaluable assistance in designing and executing various projects in this book, and for the countless hours of painstaking labor spent in completing many of the design charts.

Photographs courtesy of Zachary Freyman and Joseph Ratke.

Inquiries should be addressed to Crown Publishers, Inc., 419 Park Avenue South, New York, N.Y. 10016.

Library of Congress Catalog Card Number: 73-91517
Printed in the United States of America
Published simultaneously in Canada by
General Publishing Company Limited

Design by Nedda Balter

Contents

Plate 1. A comparison of needlepoint (right front), *canvas embroidery* (right rear), *embroidery* (left rear), *and counted thread embroidery* (left front).

Chapter 1

Materials and Methods

INTRODUCTION
WHAT IS NEEDLEPOINT?

Probably the most obvious and frequently asked question is, "What is needle-point?" Basically, it is a method of completely covering a piece of evenly woven, open-mesh fabric, called canvas, with yarn. The yarn is stitched in specific patterns through the openings of the canvas with a tapestry needle. The result is a completely new fabric which usually consists of small, diagonal, identically shaped stitches. While there are many stitch patterns, the most common covers the intersection of the horizontal and vertical canvas threads and slants from lower left to upper right. This stitch is known as the Continental, Tent, or Half Cross Stitch. The placement of the variously colored stitches results in a pattern or design on the surafce of the canvas.

Needlepoint differs from counted thread embroidery in that the background of counted thread embroidery is not completely covered with stitches. The fabric is an integral, visible part of the design. The backing fabric of counted thread embroidery is generally of a finer weave than needlepoint canvas. However, as with needlepoint, the stitches are evenly spaced and follow a prescribed direction or slant.

Embroidery differs from both needlepoint and counted thread embroidery in that the many different stitches do not rely on an evenly woven background fabric for their structure. Stitches flow freely and are more randomly placed.

The traditional background fabric, linen, is so finely woven that it is next to impossible to follow the weave of the individual threads. As with counted thread embroidery, the background fabric is usually not entirely covered by stitches.

Canvas embroidery is a combination of needlepoint and embroidery stitches worked on needlepoint canvas. The needlepoint stitches follow the patterns prescribed by the canvas while the embroidery stitches are free to roam across the canvas at will. The embroidery stitches are worked in such a manner as to cover the canvas completely. Frequently the embroidery stitches are worked on top of finished needlepoint stitches and serve as design accents or give added texture to the otherwise smooth surface of the needlepoint.

THE PURPOSE OF THIS BOOK

In this book, we have tried to provide the reader with many of the designs that we have found to be popular in our years of designing and selling needle-point canvases and kits. The designs range from the more traditional to amus-ingly whimsical. A variety of uses for each has been provided, together with appropriate instructions on how to make each project. Basic materials and methods have been thoroughly explored. Also included are the actual design charts, a large selection of stitches, and a listing of all material required for each design. It is hoped that both the novice and more experienced needle-pointer will be inspired and challenged.

CANVAS

There are two basic kinds of canvas, single thread (Mono) and double thread (Penelope). Sold by the yard, they are available in widths of from 18" to 54".

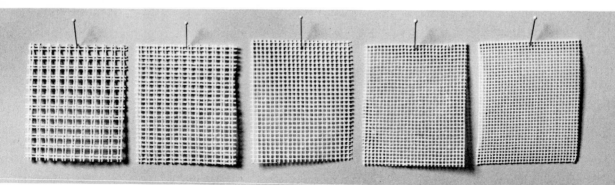

Plate 2. Penelope and Mono canvas vary greatly in size. From left to right, 4 mesh Penelope, 5 mesh Penelope, 10 mesh Mono, 12 mesh Mono, and 14 mesh Mono.

Mono Canvas

Mono canvas has no distinction between the vertical and horizontal threads. Both the vertical and horizontal threads are of the same diameter and all threads are spaced the same distance from one another. Certain stitches, such as the Half Cross, cannot be satisfactorily worked on Mono canvas. Mono canvas is also known as French, unimesh, congress, or unicanvas.

2

Penelope Canvas

Penelope canvas differs from Mono canvas in that both the vertical and horizontal threads are woven in pairs. Generally the vertical pair of threads are spaced very close together, often side by side. The horizontal pair of threads are more evenly spaced, one from the other. For most needlepoint stitches, the pair of vertical threads are considered a single thread, and the pair of horizontal threads are considered a single thread. Because the pairs of vertical threads interlock with the pairs of horizontal threads wherever they cross, Penelope canvas generally provides a firmer basis than Mono canvas.

Projects in this book may be worked on either Mono or Penelope canvas with equal results.

Quality

Since the canvas is the basis of all needlepoint and will be subjected to considerable strain during the needlepointing, blocking, and eventual use, check these quality control points:

First, the threads should be strong. If an individual thread breaks in your hand, it will probably break during blocking or will not stand much wear and tear.

Second, the threads should be straight, evenly spaced, and run at right angles to one another. If not, it will be impossible to make even stitches on a crooked background fabric.

Third, there should be a smooth, even glaze to the threads. This indicates that the threads have been treated to keep them in proper position. Also, a smooth polished finish will allow the yarn to pass freely through the holes with a minimum of wear and tear. Inferior canvas threads are frequently treated heavily with starch which will wear off during the needlepointing leaving you with a limp, lifeless gauze.

Fourth, canvas should be free of knots, broken threads, and of course, holes. While these can be repaired, anything that weakens the basic fabric should be avoided. A knot or repaired hole is usually noticeable since it is difficult to cover with the same size stitches.

Mesh Size

Canvas is measured in "mesh" sizes. This size refers to the number of threads per linear inch. For example, a 10 mesh Mono canvas has 10 single threads per inch. A 10 mesh Penelope canvas has *10 pairs*, or 20 threads per inch. Petit point generally refers to mesh sizes ranging from 40 to 14. The most popular mesh sizes are 10 and 12, and all projects in this book have been worked on 10 mesh canvas. Gros point generally refers to mesh sizes ranging from 8 to 3.

Binding Edges of Canvas

Once cut, the edges of canvas, particularly Mono, unravel with the greatest of ease. The quickest and easiest method of binding the edge of canvas is with 1" masking tape. Cut a piece the length of one side of the canvas. Apply half of the tape to the front edge and half of the tape to the back edge. Repeat on all sides. The tape will also cover the jagged edges of the canvas so that the yarn does not become snagged.

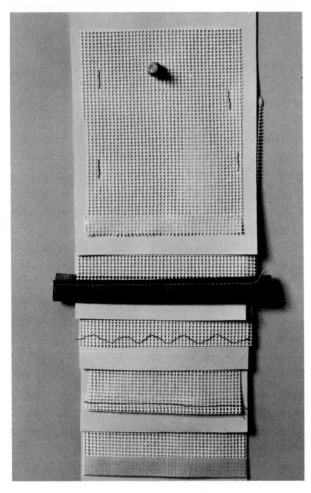

Plate 3. Canvas edges may be bound (from left to right) with glue, bias tape, zigzag stitching, straight stitching, or masking tape.

There are several alternate methods of binding the edges. Turn under ¼ ″ of canvas and stitch or glue in place. A bias tape or other cloth tape may be sewn around the edges of the canvas. A row of machine stitching will keep the canvas from unravelling, but will not cover the jagged edges.

Repairing Canvas

If you should inadvertently end up with a piece of canvas that has knots, broken threads, or holes, repair it before beginning work.

Knots will cause bumps or may come undone at a later time, leaving a hole in the face of the needlepoint. Carefully untie the knot. If the ends are long enough, overlap them side by side and apply a thin coating of upholstery glue. If the threads do not overlap sufficiently, unravel a piece of canvas thread several inches long and weave it through the mesh on either side of the broken thread, running in the same direction. Apply a thin coat of upholstery glue. Work the stitches over the broken and replacement threads. Broken canvas threads should be repaired in the same manner.

To repair a hole, trim off all frayed threads around the hole. Apply a thin coat of upholstery glue to the edge of the hole, keeping the threads in proper alignment. Cut a patch of the same size mesh, several inches larger than the hole. Apply a thin coat of upholstery glue to the edges of the patch. Place the patch under the hole. Align the canvas threads and work the stitches through both layers of canvas. Try to maintain the same tension on the stitches as you cross the patched area.

YARNS

Second in importance only to the canvas is the quality of the yarn. Needlepoint is traditionally worked with tapestry or Persian yarn. However, there are many other yarns that will produce satisfactory results and, in specific instances, may be preferred to tapestry and Persian yarns.

Plate 4. Yarns suitable for needlepoint include 4-ply rug yarns, tapestry yarns, 3-ply Persian yarns, and knitting yarns.

Persian Yarn

The aristocrat of all yarns is 3-ply Persian yarn. The most versatile and longest wearing, it is available in more shades than any other yarn. The wool is manufactured with 3 distinct threads, or ply, which can be separated or combined at will, making it possible to vary the weight or color of the yarn. Generally, 3-ply Persian yarn will cover 10 or 12 mesh canvas. The yarn is sold in various size skeins, by the ounce or even by single strands. Persian yarn has very little elasticity, making it easy to produce an even tension in each stitch. The long, tough fibers make it exceptionally strong and very long wearing. Most are mothproofed.

Tapestry Yarn

Tapestry yarn is a tough, long-wearing yarn usually sold in 40-yard skeins. Its tight twist and very long fibers make it particularly suited for the beginner since it will not separate or tangle easily. However, the long, tightly twisted fibers cannot be easily separated or combined for different weights or colors. As manufactured, it will cover 10 mesh canvas. The color range is very limited since it is primarily used as a background yarn. Most tapestry yarn is moth-proofed.

Knitting Yarn

The chief advantage of knitting yarn is that it is available almost everywhere in a wide selection of colors, and is the least expensive of the yarns mentioned. A single strand of 4-ply knitting yarn will usually cover 10 mesh canvas. However, there are two main disadvantages. First, because of its elasticity it is more difficult to maintain an even tension on the stitches. Also, if the stitches are pulled tight the canvas may be pulled completely out of shape and no amount of blocking will return it to its original shape. Second, the yarn may shed. Taking these two problems into consideration, there are many projects that can use this readily available, inexpensive yarn.

Length of Yarn Strands

Individual strands of yarn should be no longer than 24". If the strands are longer than this they become tangled. Also, the friction of the yarn as it passes through the canvas tends to remove fibers from the yarn, making the strand thinner as you progress.

Colorfastness and Dye Lots

The yarns must be colorfast. If not, the colors will run into one another during blocking or cleaning and the entire project will be ruined. Also, while working the project, the moisture from your hands may cause the colors to run.

Dye lots vary considerably, so always purchase the required quantity of a color at one time from the same dye lot. This is particularly important for large areas of color or background colors. If in doubt, purchase a little extra.

Threading the Needle

If you have difficulty threading a tapestry needle, even with its elongated eye, try one of the following techniques.

First, fold the yarn over the needle. Press this loop firmly between the thumb and forefinger. Carefully slide the needle out of the loop, maintaining pressure on the loop. Slip the loop through the eye of the needle.

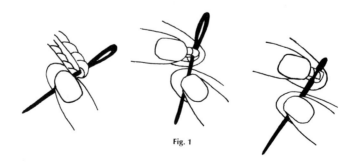

Fig. 1

Second, cut a piece of paper 3″ long and slightly narrower than the eye of the needle. Fold the paper in half. Insert one end of yarn between the paper folds. Slip the fold through the eye of the needle. Pull the paper and yarn all the way through the eye of the needle.

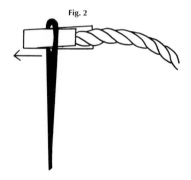

Fig. 2

Third, cut a piece of paper 3″ long and slightly narrower than the eye of the needle. Fold the paper in half. Insert the fold of the paper into the eye of the needle and push the paper *halfway* through the eye of the needle. Slip the yarn down through the fold in the paper. Pull the paper *back through the eye of the needle,* pulling the yarn with it.

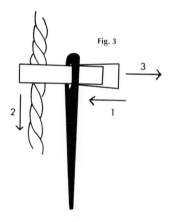

Fig. 3

Fourth, small wire and/or plastic yarn threaders are available at needle-work, notion, and variety stores. Push the wire loop through the eye of the needle. Slip the yarn through the wire loop and pull the wire loop and yarn back through the eye of the needle.

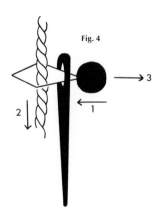

Fig. 4

Beginning and Ending Yarn

Knots are not used to begin or end yarn since a knot on the back of the needlepoint will make a lump on the face of the needlepoint.

One method of beginning with a fresh canvas is to bring the needle up through the canvas at the beginning of the first stitch, leaving about 1″ of yarn on the back of the canvas. Hold this 1″ end of yarn against the back of the canvas and secure it with the first 4 to 6 stitches.

Fig. 5

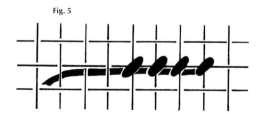

A "waste knot" may also be used. Knot one end of the yarn and carry it down through the face of the canvas so that the knot will be in the direct line of stitches, 5 or 6 meshes from the point where you intend to begin stitching. Bring the needle up through the canvas at the starting point and catch the yarn to the back of the canvas with the first few stitches. Clip off the knot and the excess yarn from the back of the canvas. Instead of a knot, the yarn may be woven through several meshes directly in front of the first few stitches.

Fig. 6

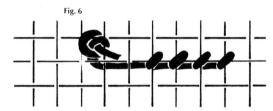

Once some stitches have been worked, each succeeding piece of yarn should be woven through the back of several stitches close to where you intend to begin needlepointing. Similarly, the yarn should be ended by weaving it through the back of several nearby stitches. Begin and end each succeeding row at a different point on the canvas or a ridge will develop on the face of the canvas.

Fig. 7

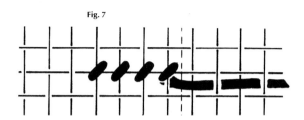

To begin or end yarn at either side of the background area, simply weave the yarn through several meshes outside the background area. This will eliminate unnecessary bulk at the edges of the background.

When working around small areas of finished stitches, it is permissible to skip across the back of the finished stitches rather than end on one side and begin anew on the other side. These skips should be no longer than 1″.

Tension

One of the great beauties of needlepoint is that all the stitches are identical and present a smooth, uniform surface. Proper tension is the key factor. Each stitch should be pulled with the same amount of tension as all the others. If they are too loose they will snag. If they are too tight the canvas will show through and will be stretched completely out of shape. Practice is the only answer to this problem. For the novice, a concerted effort should be made to keep each stitch just as tight as its predecessor. Eventually, it will become a habit.

Removing Stitches

Removing stitches is probably the most tedious and frustrating of all aspects of needlepoint. If only a few stitches have to be removed, unthread the needle and with the point pull them out, one by one, starting with the last stitch. Do not try to needlepoint backwards because you will only succeed in stitching through the back of adjoining stitches, making a hopeless tangle. If a larger area has to be removed, the stitches may be cut out (see *Scissors*).

Color Selection

Exact colors and shadings should be determined by personal preference and the specific requirements of the room. Keep the following points in mind when selecting colors:

First, the colors should harmonize with one another. Unless a specific highlight is desired, no one color should appear stronger than its neighbors. A good way to check this is to lay the colors side by side. If one seems to stand out from the rest, it is probably too strong.

Second, select colors that will either harmonize or accent those surrounding it in the room where it is to be used. Take into consideration the chair and sofa covers, draperies, rugs, etc. If possible, take fabric or paint swatches when selecting yarns.

Third, yarn in skeins appears much brighter than when finally worked up into needlepoint. This is because the large exposure of the skeins allows you to see a large splash of color. When the skeins are worked up, your eye sees only small spots of color from each stitch.

NEEDLES

Special needles, called tapestry needles, are used for needlepoint. They have blunt points and elongated eyes. The blunt points make it easy to avoid splitting canvas threads, and the elongated eyes are necessary to accommodate the relatively thick needlepoint yarns. They are available in various sizes, numbered from 13 to 24, the larger number being the smaller needle. Number 18 was used on the 10 mesh canvas for all the projects in this book. Number 13 is commonly called a rug needle and is used on numbers 3, 4, and 5 mesh canvas. When choosing a needle size, remember that the needle should be small enough to pass through the mesh of the canvas easily, and the eye should be large enough to accommodate the yarn. Tapestry needles are usually sold in packages containing various sizes. It is advisable to purchase some extra since they have a way of disappearing at the most inopportune times. Plastic pill bottles make admirable storage containers.

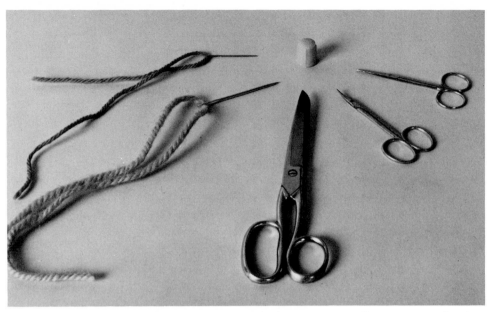

Plate 5. The tools needed for needlepoint include tapestry needles, scissors of various sizes, and perhaps a thimble.

THIMBLES

A thimble is very much a matter of personal preference. If you are a confirmed needlepointer, or if you work on a frame, you may find that some form of protection is required. Thimbles are available in plastic and metal, and since they come in different sizes and weights, be sure to try them on before purchasing one.

SCISSORS

All scissors should be very sharp, since dull scissors will result in frayed canvas, yarn, and patience. Several different sizes will be helpful. A medium-sized all-purpose scissors will be useful for cutting canvas and full skeins of yarn. While working, small embroidery scissors are useful for cutting individual strands and ends of yarn. For cutting out stitches, use special stitch-cutting scissors or curved manicure scissors. The stitch-cutting scissors has, near the point of one of the blades, a small circular cutout portion that slips under a single stitch, cutting it out with little danger of cutting the canvas. The point of a curved manicure scissors will slide under several stitches, but there is more danger of cutting the canvas.

FRAMES

Needlepoint does not *require* the use of a frame of any kind. However, without a frame, canvas becomes crooked because of handling and because the stitches pull the canvas out of shape. A frame will keep the canvas straight and facilitate its handling. The chief disadvantages of a frame are that the project is much less portable and it may require two separate motions to complete a single stitch. Embroidery hoops are of limited application because the bulk of the canvas and finished stitches will not fit between the two hoops.

Plate 6. A frame of artist stretchers (rear) or a rolling needlepoint frame (front) will keep the canvas straight during the needlepointing and eliminate the need for blocking afterwards.

Rolling Needlepoint Frames

The most practical frame is the type that consists of two rollers, one in front and one in back, joined by supports on either side. The canvas is attached to the two rollers and the portions of canvas which are not being worked, or which have been completed, are rolled out of the way. These frames are available with various length rods to accommodate various sizes of canvas. Small frames are held with one hand, leaving the other hand free to needlepoint. Larger frames are available with legs and are completely freestanding, leaving both hands free to needlepoint.

Artist Stretchers and Lath Frames

Artist stretchers are slotted wood frames which are normally covered with canvas. They are inexpensive and come in 1" lengths from several inches long to several feet long making different size frames possible. Canvas is tacked or stapled to the frame leaving the entire design visible. Keep the tacks or staples outside the background area or they may stretch or break the canvas threads.

Commercially manufactured frames are available and consist of wooden slats that may be assembled, similar to artists' stretchers. One size frame will accommodate several sizes of canvas. Of course, a frame of 1" by 2" lumber will also serve the purpose. Cut the lumber large enough to fit the outside measurements of the canvas. Secure the corners with flat 1" brackets, and tack or staple the outside edge of the canvas to the frame.

Rolling frames, artists' stretchers, and lath frames are easily assembled, disassembled, and may be stored in a minimum of space.

GLUE

Use a high-quality upholstery glue to repair canvas and mount projects. Be sure that it is waterproof when dry so that it does not disintegrate during blocking and cleaning. It should also dry clear so that any spillage or over-saturation will not be noticed. The glue should be flexible when dry; otherwise the canvas will become stiff and the glue will crack and chip off.

TACKS, STAPLES, OR PUSHPINS

Rustproof tacks, staples, or pushpins should be used for blocking and mounting needlepoint. If not, water applied to needlepoint during blocking will cause rust spots. Also, natural humidity may eventually cause rust spots on mounted needlepoint.

ENLARGING AND REDUCING DESIGNS

Designs have been applied to specific projects. If you decide that you have an alternate use for a design, but the size is incorrect, there are several methods of changing the size.

Photostats

Place a piece of tracing paper over the chart and carefully outline the design. Ask a firm that specializes in photostats for a positive stat the size you desire. The new design will have exactly the same proportions as the original and may be larger or smaller than the original. Trace the design on canvas using a permanent felt tip pen.

Graph Method

To enlarge a design, place a piece of tracing paper over the chart and carefully outline the design. Mark the tracing into squares or rectangles, ⅛" for small designs, and ¼, ½, or 1" for larger designs. On a second paper, outline the area you want the new design to occupy. The new design size must be in the same proportion as the original. Divide the new design area into the same number and sequence of squares or rectangles as the original. Simply copy the design from the smaller squares to the corresponding larger squares. To reduce a design, reverse the process.

Fig. 8

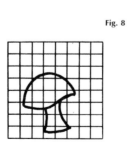
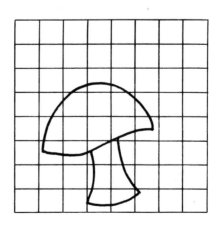

Changing Mesh Size

All projects have been worked on 10 mesh canvas. To enlarge a design, simply follow the chart and substitute a larger mesh canvas. Conversely, to reduce a design, simply follow the chart and substitute a smaller mesh canvas. Remember that, in changing mesh size, yarn requirements and stitches will have to be altered to fit the new size canvas.

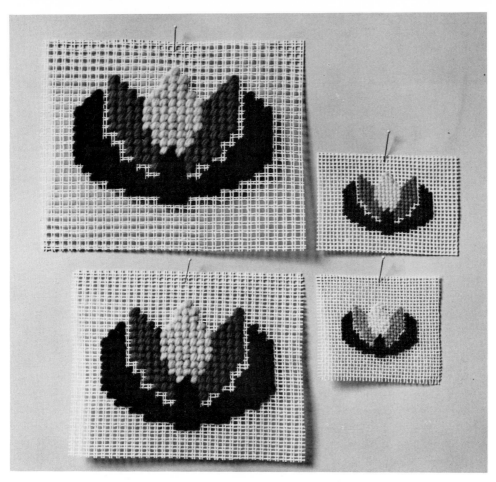

Plate 7. Designs may be varied in size by working them on various size canvases. Here the same design is worked on 3 mesh Penelope (upper left), *5 mesh Penelope* (lower left), *10 mesh Mono* (upper right), *and 12 mesh Mono* (lower right).

WORKING FROM A CHART

All projects in this book have been reproduced in chart form enabling you to duplicate the design as shown. The lines on the chart serve as a counting aid to show the placement of the individual stitches and color areas. Each chart contains several symbols and numbers representing different colors and stitches. Each stitch has been indicated by a symbol in small design areas. In larger areas, the colors have been outlined with a single row of symbols or line. Once this outline row has been worked, the number inside will indicate the colors and stitches to be used for filling in the area.

First, determine the canvas size required by adding 1½ to 2″ to the design size, *on all sides.* The design size in the key includes only the design and a suggested background area. It does not allow for the margin around the background necessary for blocking. Also, large areas of background are not indicated on individual charts. Find the center of the canvas. Lacking a ruler, fold the canvas in half horizontally. Then fold the canvas in half vertically. The point where the two folds intersect will be the center. Mark it with a pin or needle. The center of each chart is marked with a heavy cross. Determine which stitches are in the center, or nearest the center. Begin working the design from this spot, or as near as possible, making a stitch to correspond to each symbol on the chart. Continue the design, working from the completed stitches until the entire design in completed or outlined. After the outlined portions of the design have been filled in, outline and work the background area.

13

Chart Sampler Pincushion

(4½″ by 4½″. Fig. 9 and Plate 8)

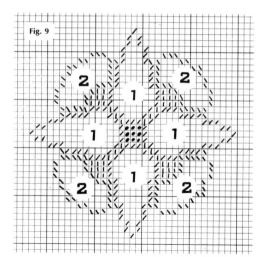

Colors and Stitches:

- ● Yellow Continental No. 1
- ╱ Light Pink Continental No. 1
- ╲ Dark Pink Continental No. 1
- I Red Continental No. 1
- 1 Light Pink Continental No. 1
- 2 Dark Pink Continental No. 1

Background Red and Black Scotch No. 1

Yarn Requirements:

Yellow—¼ yard
Light Pink—6 yards
Dark Pink—6 yards
Red—4 yards
Black—3 yards

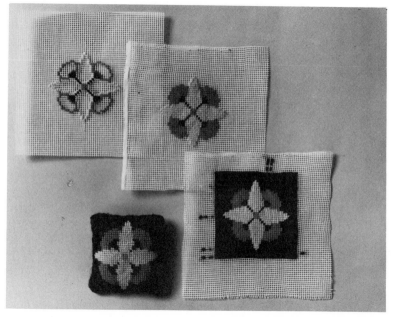

Plate 8. When working from a chart, outline the design (upper left); fill in the design (upper right); fill in the background (lower right); and finally make the finished needlepoint into the finished product.

GENERAL WORKING CONDITIONS

For this time-consuming craft, use a comfortable, upholstered chair with adequate back support and plenty of seat room on either side to hold your yarn and scissors. Adequate light is a must. A combination of overall general light and a directional, high-intensity lighting is ideal. Keep everything clean and readily accessible by storing all your materials in a large, lightweight container, such as a lined wicker basket or hatbox. Store individual skeins of yarn in plastic bags. Yarns may be kept tangle-free if all the strands of one color are loosely knotted together in the center. Pull individual strands from the knot without disturbing the entire bundle. Do not distort canvas by folding or crumpling. Roll the portion not being worked and secure the rolls with paper clips or safety pins.

Chapter 2

Designs and Charts

The designs in this chapter have been divided into various categories, depending upon their subject matter, and are meant to fit almost any decor and decorating situation. The design categories are: 1. Abstracts and Graphics; 2. Ladybugs, Butterflies, and Birds; 3. Hearts and Flowers; 4. Fruit and Mushrooms; 5. Nursery and Whimsical; 6. Classical and Repeat Designs; 7. Designs Inspired by Nature; and 8. Zodiacs. The designs have been adapted to various projects, and complete mounting and finishing instructions follow this chapter. Many designs have alternate uses suggested, and the only limitation for endless application of these designs is your imagination.

Scallop Sunburst Wall Hanging
(15'' by 15''. Fig. 10 and Plate 9)

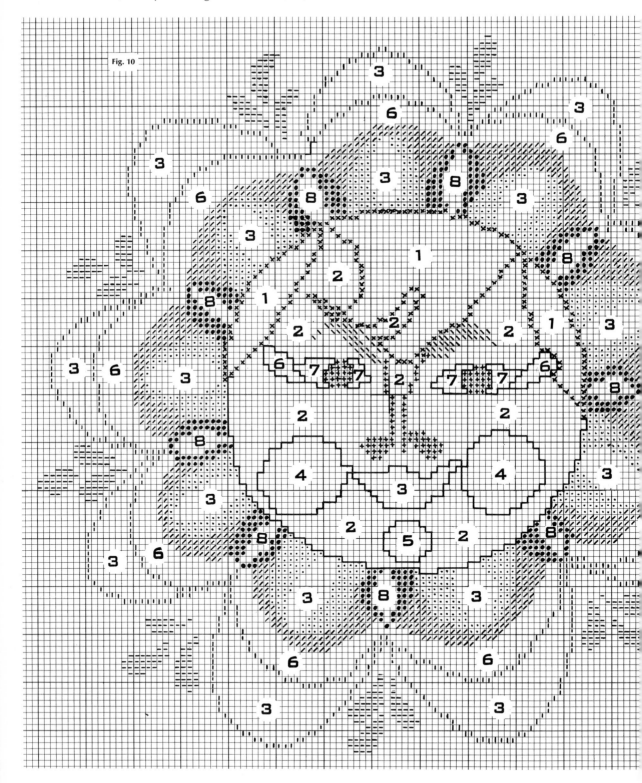

Colors and Stitches:

× Gold Continental No. 1
I Red Continental No. 1
− Shocking Pink
   Continental No. 1
• Light Pink Continental No. 1
● Light Blue Continental No. 1
╱ Dark Blue Continental No. 1
+ Black Continental No. 1
╲ Dark Purple Continental No. 1
1 Gold Basketweave No. 1
2 Yellow Basketweave No. 1
3 Red Basketweave No. 1
4 Shocking Pink
   Basketweave No. 1
5 Light Pink Basketweave No. 1
6 Light Purple Basketweave No. 1
7 White Basketweave No. 1
8 Dark Purple Basketweave No. 1
  Background Eggshell
   Basketweave No. 1

Yarn Requirements:

Gold—8 yards
Red—30 yards
Shocking Pink—13 yards
Light Pink—13 yards
Light Blue—9 yards
Dark Blue—15 yards
Black—1 yard
Dark Purple—6 yards
Yellow—15 yards
Light Purple—18 yards
White—¾ yard
Eggshell—110 yards

Plate 9. The Scallop Sunburst Wall Hanging would be equally appropriate as a pillow or upholstery piece. The bright, cheery face would brighten any living room, den, or family room.

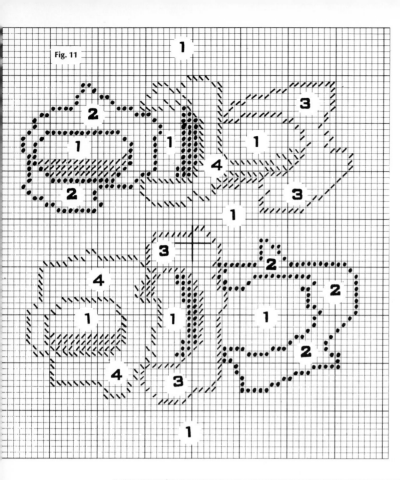

Abstract No. 1 Wall Hanging
(7" by 7". Fig. 11 and Plate 10)

Colors and Stitches:

- • Red Continental No. 1
- / Turquoise Continental No. 1
- \ Purple Continental No. 1
- 1 Yellow Basketweave No. 1
- 2 Red Basketweave No. 1
- 3 Turquoise Basketweave No. 1
- 4 Purple Basketweave No. 1

Yarn Requirements:

Red—8 yards
Turquoise—8 yards
Purple—8 yards
Yellow—30 yards

Abstract No. 2 Wall Hanging
(7" by 7". Fig. 12 and Plate 10)

Colors and Stitches:

- • Yellow Continental No. 1
- / Blue Continental No. 1
- \ White Continental No. 1
- I Red Continental No. 1
- − Orange Continental No. 1
- 1 Yellow Basketweave No. 1
- 2 Blue Basketweave No. 1
- 3 Red Basketweave No. 1
- 4 Orange Basketweave No. 1
  Background Brown
    Basketweave No. 1

Yarn Requirements:

Yellow—10 yards
Blue—8 yards
White—¼ yard
Red—6 yards
Orange—4 yards
Brown—25 yards

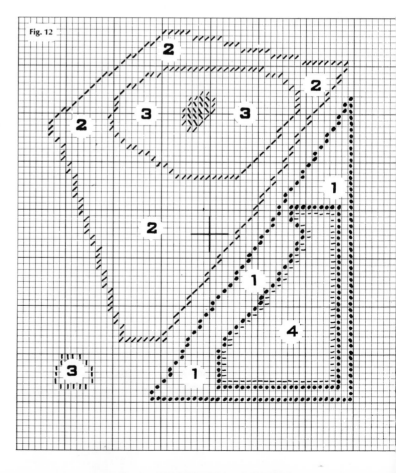

18

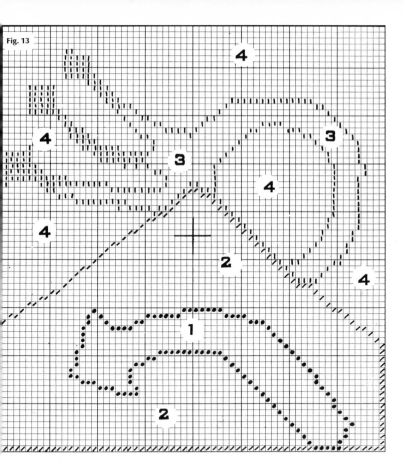

Fig. 13

Abstract No. 3 Wall Hanging

(7'' by 7''. Fig. 13 and Plate 10)

Colors and Stitches:

- ● Turquoise Continental No. 1
- ╱ Shocking Pink
   Continental No. 1
- Ι Green Continental No. 1
- 1 Turquoise Basketweave No. 1
- 2 Shocking Pink
   Basketweave No. 1
- 3 Green Basketweave No. 1
- 4 Yellow Basketweave No. 1

Yarn Requirements:

Turquoise—6 yards
Shocking Pink—18 yards
Green—18 yards
Yellow—8 yards

Plate 10. Abstract Nos. 1, 2, and 3 have been double mounted on a leather-covered backing board to form this handsome wall panel. The designs would also be effective if hung individually.

Cube Graphic Pillow
(12″ by 11″. Fig. 14 and Plate 11)

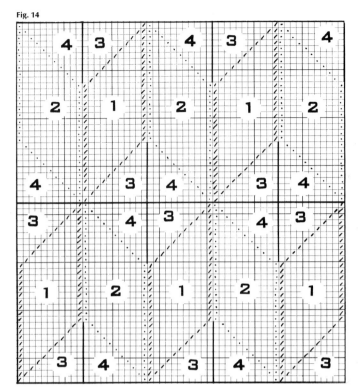

Fig. 14

Colors and Stitches:

/ Light Rust Continental No. 1
• Dark Rust Continental No. 2
1 Light Rust Scotch No. 1
2 Dark Rust Scotch No. 2
3 Brown Continental No. 1
4 Brown Continental No. 2

Yarn Requirements:

Light Rust—60 yards
Dark Rust—60 yards
Brown—24 yards

Plate 11. The design of the Cube Graphic Pillow is further enhanced by the use of diagonally opposing stitches, such as the Scotch No. 1 and No. 2 and the Continental No. 1 and No. 2.

Tick-Tack-Toe Pincushion or Sachet
(5″ by 5″. Fig. 15 and Plate 12)

Colors and Stitches:

/ Blue Continental No. 1
1 Light Purple Scotch No. 1
2 Red Scotch No. 1
3 Working from the Blue toward the outside, add 1 row of each of the following:
   Light Pink Continental No. 1; Dark Purple Continental No. 1; Gold Continental No. 1; Yellow Stem No. 1 and Slanting Gobelin No. 4; Light Purple Stem No. 1 and Slanting Gobelin No. 4
4 Red and Pink Scotch No. 1 Alternating
5 Dark Purple Stem No. 1 and Slanting Gobelin No. 4

Yarn Requirements:
Red—4 yards
Light Purple—4 yards
Dark Purple—6 yards
Yellow—4 yards
Gold—4 yards
Blue—3 yards
Pink—4 yards

Fig. 15

Diamond Pincushion
(4½″ by 4½″. Fig. 16 and Plate 12)

Colors and Stitches:

1 Pink Scotch No. 1
2 Green Scotch No. 1
3 Gold Scotch No. 1
4 Blue Scotch No. 1
5 Rows of Yellow, Pink, Gold, Blue, Light Purple Continental No. 1
  6 Rows of Pink, Green, Gold Stem No. 1 and Slanting Gobelin No. 3
• Green Continental No. 1
/ Light Purple and Dark Purple Scotch No. 1 Alternating
  Light Purple Stem No. 3 and Slanting Gobelin No. 1
Work 1 row of Dark Purple Stem No. 3 and Slanting Gobelin No. 1 around the outside edge.

Yarn Requirements:

Pink—4 yards
Green—4 yards
Gold—4 yards
Blue—3 yards
Yellow—4 yards
Light Purple—4 yards
Dark Purple—4 yards

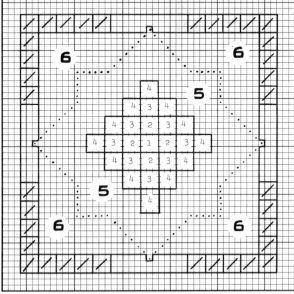

Fig. 16

Stars and Stripes Eyeglass Case or Checkbook Cover

(4″ by 7″. Fig. 17 and Plate 12)

Colors and Stitches:

- ● White Continental No. 1
- ╱ Red Continental No. 1
- • Blue Continental No. 1
- 1 White Basketweave No. 1
- 2 Red Basketweave No. 1
- 3 Blue Basketweave No. 1

Yarn Requirements for One Side:

Red—10 yards
White—10 yards
Blue—10 yards

Plate 12. Small bazaar items such as the Tick-Tack-Toe Pincushion or Sachet (upper left), Diamond Pincushion or Sachet (upper right), and the Stars and Stripes Eyeglass Case or Checkbook Cover make excellent gifts since they are very quickly made and may be done with odds and ends of yarn—each color requiring a very small quantity of yarn.

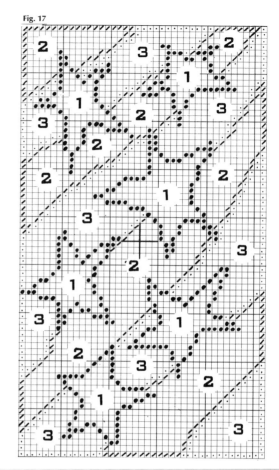

Fig. 17

22

Square Sampler Pillow

(10″ by 10″. Fig. 18 and Plate 13)

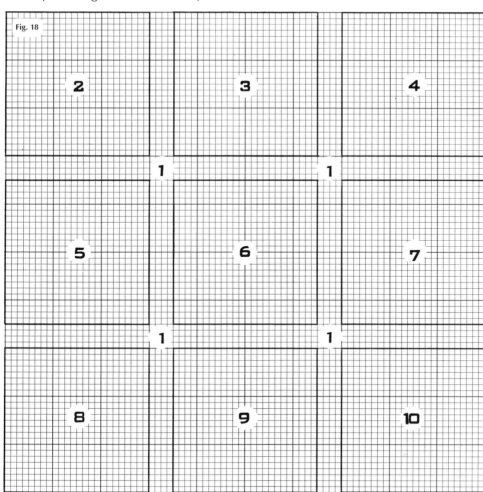

Fig. 18

Colors and Stitches:

1. Black Continental No. 1
2. Light Pink Scotch No. 1
3. Medium Rose Straight Gobelin
4. Light Pink Diagonal Cashmere
5. Dark Pink Brick
6. Dark Rose Straight Cross
7. Dark Pink Stem No. 5
8. Light Pink Diagonal Mosaic No. 1
9. Medium Rose Slanting Gobelin No. 4
10. Light Pink Mosaic No. 1
    Work 4 rows of Black Continental No. 1 around the outside edge. Work 4 rows of Gray Slanting Gobelin No. 3 and Stem No. 2 around the black.

Yarn Requirements:

Black—32 yards
Gray—23 yards
Light Pink—22 yards
Dark Pink—17 yards
Medium Rose—20 yards
Dark Rose—8 yards

Plate 13. The Square Sampler Pillow consists of 12 basic needle-point stitches; Continental No. 1, Scotch No. 1, Mosaic No. 1, Diagonal Mosaic No. 1, Diagonal Cashmere, Straight Cross, Brick, Straight Gobelin, Slanting Gobelin No. 3, Slanting Gobelin No. 4, Stem No. 2, and Stem No. 5.

Graphic Square Pillow

(10½″ by 10½″. Fig. 19 and Plate 14)

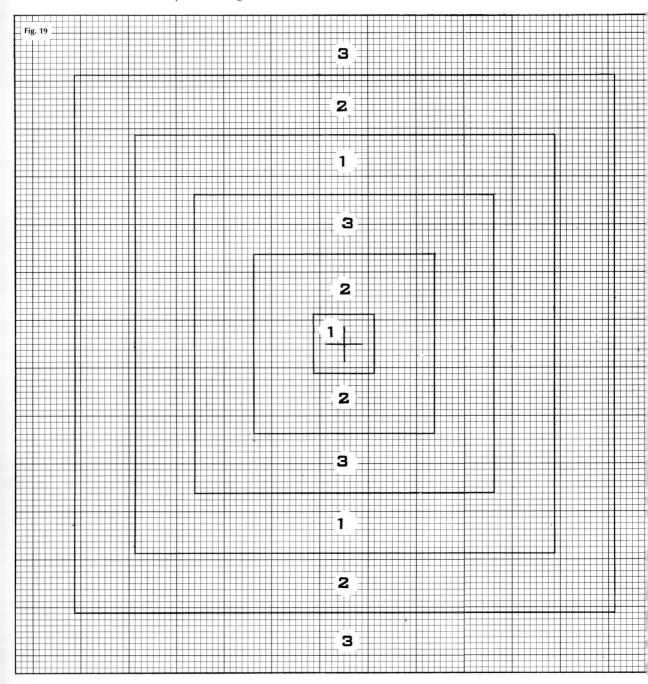

Fig. 19

Colors and Stitches:
1 Red Basketweave No. 1
2 White Basketweave No. 1
3 Blue Basketweave No. 1

Yarn Requirements:
Red—40 yards
White—40 yards
Blue—40 yards

Peace Symbol Pillow

(10'' by 9''. Fig. 20 and Plate 14)

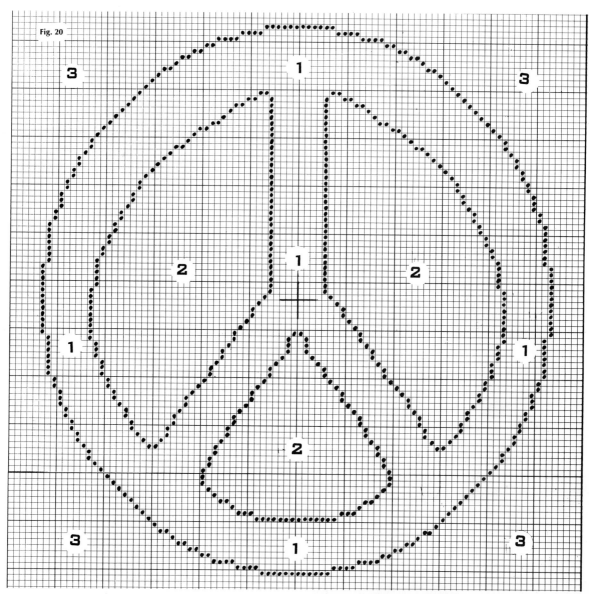

Fig. 20

Colors and Stitches:

- ● White Continental No. 1
- 1 White Basketweave No. 1
- 2 Red Basketweave No. 1
- 3 Blue Basketweave No. 1

Yarn Requirements:

Red—30 yards
White—30 yards
Blue—30 yards

Plate 14. A basic red, white, and blue theme has been used in the Peace Symbol Pillow (top), Stars and Stripes Pillow (left) and Graphic Square Pillow (right).

Stars and Stripes Pillow

(11½″ by 9″. Fig. 21 and Plate 14)

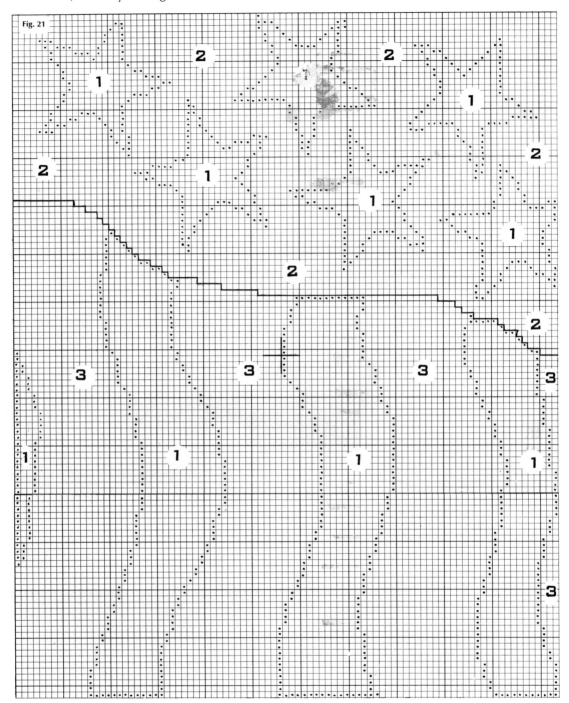

Colors and Stitches:

- White Continental No. 1
1 White Basketweave No. 1
2 Blue Basketweave No. 1
3 Red Basketweave No. 1

Yarn Requirements:

Red—35 yards
White—35 yards
Blue—35 yards

COLOR PLATE 1

See keyed diagrams on pages 199 and 200 for explanation of each item in these color plates.

COLOR PLATE 2

COLOR PLATE 3

COLOR PLATE 4

COLOR PLATE 5

COLOR PLATE 6

COLOR PLATE 7

COLOR PLATE 8

Rectangles Sachet or Pincushion

(3¾″ by 4¾″. Fig. 22 and Plate 15)

Fig. 22

1	2	3	2	6	2	3	2	1
3	5	1	10	11	10	1	5	3
2	4	13	9	12	9	13	4	2
8	9	5	3	10	3	5	9	8
7	14	15	16	17	16	15	14	7
8	9	5	3	10	3	5	9	8
2	4	13	9	12	9	13	4	2
3	5	1	10	11	10	1	5	3
1	2	3	2	6	2	3	2	1

11 Two Blue Cashmere No. 2
12 Two Pink Cashmere No. 2
13 Shocking Pink Slanting Gobelin No. 2
14 Four Blue Cashmere No. 2
15 Four Pink Cashmere No. 2
16 Four Purple Cashmere No. 2
17 Four Shocking Pink Cashmere No. 2

Yarn Requirements:

Red—8 yards
Blue—1½ yards
Pink—2 yards
Yellow—1 yard
Purple—1½ yards
Orange—1 yard
Shocking Pink—1½ yards
Green—1¼ yards

Colors and Stitches:

Work heavy lines with Red Continental No. 2.

Fill each rectangle with the following:

1 Blue Slanting Gobelin No. 2
2 Pink Continental No. 1
3 Yellow Continental No. 1
4 Purple Continental No. 1
5 Two Orange Cashmere No. 2
6 Two Yellow Cashmere No. 2
7 Four Yellow Cashmere No. 2
8 Two Shocking Pink Cashmere No. 2
9 Two Green Cashmere No. 2
10 Two Purple Cashmere No. 2

Plate 15. The Rectangles Pincushion or Sachet (left) is excellent for using up those very small leftover pieces of yarn since the squares can be worked completely ar random. The Union Jack Pincushion or Sachet (right) was inspired by the British flag and is an fine example of using various stitches to form a design.

Union Jack Sachet or Pincushion

(5" by 5". Fig. 23 and Plate 15)

Fig. 23

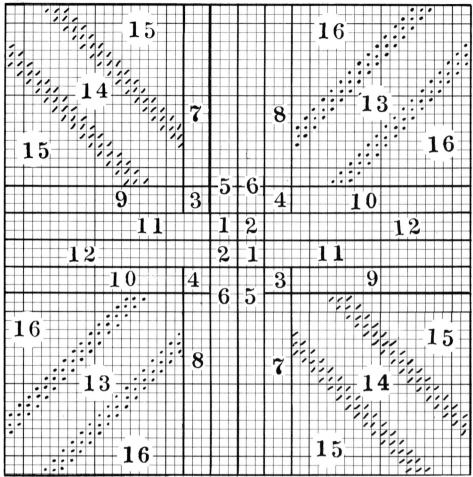

Colors and Stitches:

Work from the center of the design
to the outside of the design.
- • White Continental No. 2
- ╱ White Continental No. 1
- 1 Red Scotch No. 1
- 2 Red Scotch No. 2
- 3 White Scotch No. 1
- 4 White Scotch No. 2
- 5 Red Stem No. 3
- 6 Red Stem No. 4
- 7 White Stem No. 3
- 8 White Stem No. 4
- 9 White Slanting Gobelin No. 1
- 10 White Slanting Gobelin No. 2
- 11 Red Slanting Gobelin No. 1
- 12 Red Slanting Gobelin No. 2
- 13 Red Diagonal Mosaic No. 4
- 14 Red Diagonal Mosaic No. 3
- 15 Blue Diagonal Mosaic No. 1
- 16 Blue Diagonal Mosaic No. 2

Yarn Requirements:

Red—8 yards
White—10 yards
Blue—9 yards

Octagon Repeat

(13″ by 13″. Fig. 24 and Plate 16)   Designed by Rena Sherman

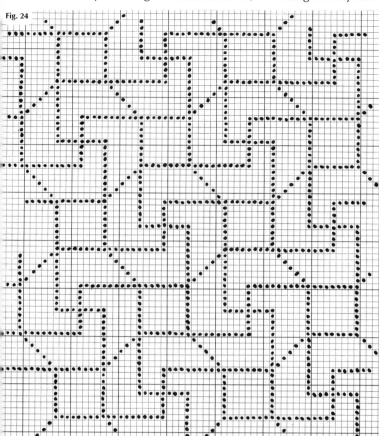

Fig. 24

Colors and Stitches:

- Black Continental No. 1
  Fill the balance of the design in with Basketweave No. 1 in miscellaneous colors, with no two adjoining areas of the same color.

Yarn Requirements:

Black—1½ yards per octagon
  ½ yard per square
Colors—¾ yard per block
  ½ yard per square

Plate 16. The Octagon Repeat is another type of design which is excellent for using leftover colors since each section of the design can be filled in with different colors, depending upon what is at hand or the color scheme desired.

Love Wall Hanging
(8½" by 10¾". Fig. 25 and Plate 17)

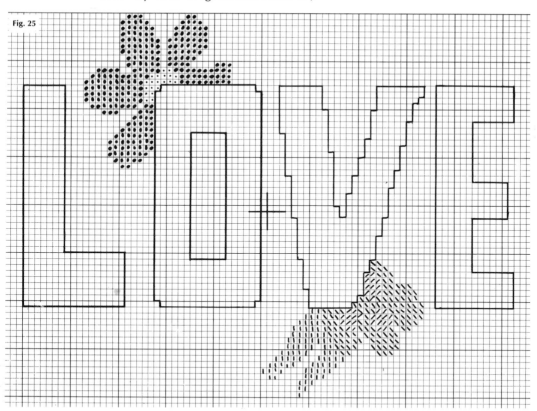

Fig. 25

Fig.

Colors and Stitches:

L Light Blue Basketweave No. 1
O Rose Basketweave No. 1
V Yellow Basketweave No. 1
E Pink Basketweave No. 1
● Orange Continental No. 1
• Yellow Continental No. 1
I Green Continental No. 1
\ Dark Rose Continental No. 1
/ Light Pink Continental No. 1
  Background Brown
    Basketweave No. 1

Yarn Requirements:

Light Blue—6 yards
Rose—8 yards
Yellow—8 yards
Pink—8 yards
Orange—4 yards
Yellow—½ yard
Green—1½ yards
Dark Rose—3 yards
Light Pink—¾ yard
Brown—55 yards

Plate 17. The Love Wall Hanging is a thoughtful gift for someone special in your life. It would be equally appropriate as a pillow or box top.

Medallion Sunburst Pillow

(16¾″ by 10½″. Fig. 26 and Plate 18)

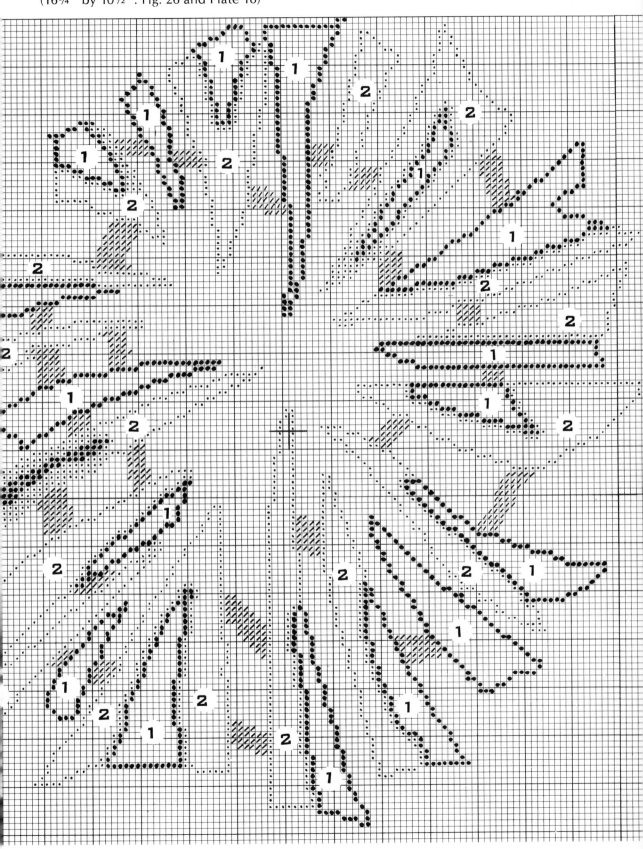

Medallion Sunburst Pillow *(continued)*

Plate 18. The Medallion Sunburst Pillow was inspired by a piece of modern abstract jewelry. Its colors could be varied to fit almost any color scheme.

Colors and Stitches:

- Light Orange Continental No. 1
- Dark Orange Continental No. 1
/ Eggshell Continental No. 1
1 Light Orange Basketweave No. 1
2 Dark Orange Basketweave No. 1
  Background Red
    Basketweave No. 1

Yarn Requirements:

Light Orange—35 yards
Dark Orange—35 yards
Eggshell—25 yards
Red—90 yards

Ladybug on Leaves Wall Hanging

(9" by 9". Fig. 27 and Plate 19)

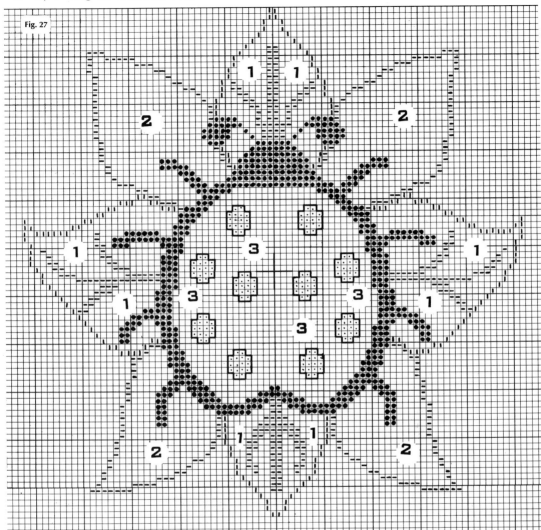

Fig. 27

Colors and Stitches:

All stitches on the right side are worked with No. 1 stitches and all stitches on the left side are worked with No. 2 stitches.

— Light Green Continental No. 1 and Continental No. 2

l Dark Green Continental No. 1 and Continental No. 2

● Black Continental No. 1 and Continental No. 2

• Black Vertical Satin

1 Dark Green Basketweave No. 1 and Basketweave No. 2

2 Light Green Basketweave No. 1 and Basketweave No. 2

3 Red Diagonal Mosaic No. 1 and Diagonal Mosaic No. 2

Background Eggshell Scotch No. 1 and Scotch No. 2

Yarn Requirements:

Light Green—8 yards
Dark Green—12 yards
Black—8 yards
Red—8 yards
Eggshell—48 yards

Butterfly on Lattice Pillow

(9" by 9". Fig. 28 and Plate 19)

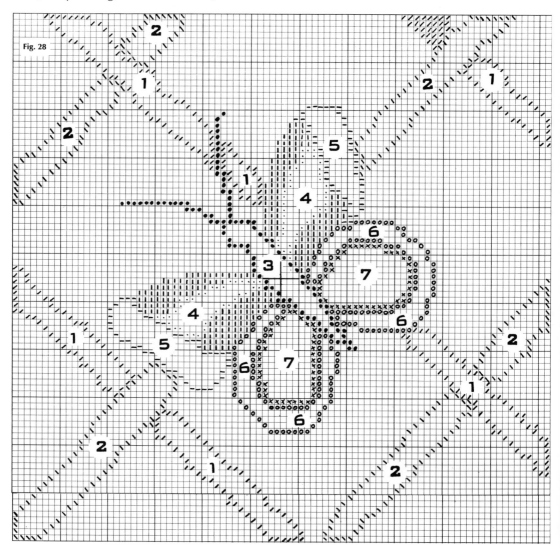

Fig. 28

Colors and Stitches:

/ Dark Gold Continental No. 1
\ Light Gold Continental No. 1
● Gray Continental No. 1
I Dark Rose Continental No. 1
• Red Continental No. 1
− Light Purple Continental No. 1
○ Light Blue Continental No. 1
× Dark Blue Continental No. 1
1 Dark Gold Basketweave No. 1
2 Light Gold Basketweave No. 1
3 Gray Basketweave No. 1
4 Red Basketweave No. 1
5 Light Purple Basketweave No. 1
6 Light Blue Basketweave No. 1
7 Dark Blue Basketweave No. 1
  Background Eggshell
    Basketweave No. 1

Yarn Requirements:

Dark Gold—16 yards
Light Gold—16 yards
Gray—4 yards
Dark Rose—4 yards
Red—3 yards
Light Purple—3 yards
Light Blue—4 yards
Dark Blue—3 yards
Eggshell—35 yards

Plate 19. The Ladybug on Leaves Wall Hanging design (right) was split down the center. All the stitches on one side slant in the reverse direction from those on the other side of the center. The Butterfly on Lattice Pillow is a example of an appliquéd pillow. The small piece of needlepoint was sewn on the face of a pillow and the raw edges of canvas were covered with moss fringe.

Wise Owl Pillow

(12″ diameter. Fig. 29 and Plate 20)

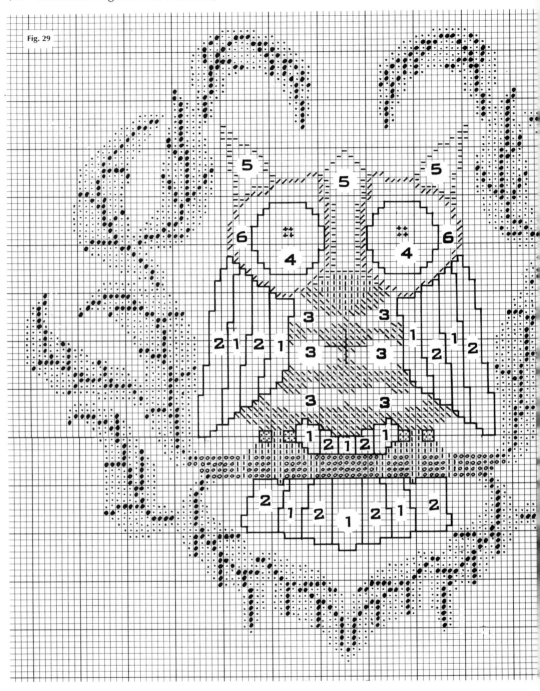

Fig. 29

Plate 20. The Wise Owl Pillow is another example of an appliquéd pillow. In this case the circular needlepoint was mounted on a square pillow resulting in added design interest.

Colors and Stitches:

- ◯ Medium Brown Continental No. 1
- ▣ Shocking Pink Continental No. 1
- + Black Continental No. 1
- ＼ Medium Blue Continental No. 1
- ● Dark Olive Continental No. 1
- • Light Olive Continental No. 1
- − Salmon Continental No. 1
- | Gold Continental No. 1
- / Light Red Continental No. 1
- 1 Shocking Pink Continental No. 1
- 2 Dark Red Continental No. 1
- 3 Light Blue Continental No. 1
- 4 White Basketweave No. 1
- 5 Salmon Basketweave No. 1
- 6 Light Red Continental No. 1
  Background Black Basketweave No. 1

Yarn Requirements:

Medium Blue—6 yards
Shocking Pink—8 yards
Black—50 yards
Medium Brown—3 yards
Dark Olive—10 yards
Light Olive—15 yards
Salmon—3 yards
Gold—1½ yards
Light Red—3 yards
Dark Red—10 yards
Light Blue—4 yards
White—4 yards

Witty Owl Pillow
(9″ diameter. Fig. 30 and Plate 21)

Fig. 30

Plate 21. The Witty Owl Pillow is a companion to the Wise Owl Pillow. In both cases the design is completely symmetrical. That is, the stitches on one side of the center match the stitches on the other side.

Colors and Stitches:

- ▦ Light Pink Continental No. 1
  Fill in the balance of the chest with Medium Pink Continental No. 1
- \ Dark Olive Continental No. 1
- • Light Olive Continental No. 1
- ● Shocking Pink Continental No. 1
- / Medium Blue Continental No. 1
- I Gold Continental No. 1
- − Brown Continental No. 1
- + Black Continental No. 1
- × Dark Red Continental No. 1
- ○ Medium Pink Continental No. 1
- 1 Light Blue Continental No. 1
- 2 Shocking Pink Continental No. 1
- 3 Medium Red Continental No. 1
- 4 Yellow Continental No. 1
- 5 White Continental No. 1
  Background Black Basketweave No. 1

Yarn Requirements:

Light Pink—6 yards
Medium Pink—6 yards
Dark Olive—10 yards
Light Olive—15 yards
Shocking Pink—6 yards
Medium Blue—12 yards
Gold—1 yard
Brown—2 yards
Black—40 yards
Dark Red—¾ yard
Light Blue—10 yards
Medium Red—3 yards
Yellow—2½ yards
White—¾ yard

39

Swirl of Butterflies Pillow
(14″ by 15″. Fig. 31 and Plate 22)

Fig. 31

Colors and Stitches:

- ○ Gold Continental No. 1
- ╱ Pink Continental No. 1
- | Black Continental No. 1
- ╲ Yellow Continental No. 1
- − Red Continental No. 1
- • Blue Continental No. 1
- 1 Gold Basketweave No. 1
- 2 Pink Basketweave No. 1
- 3 Yellow Basketweave No. 1
- 4 Red Basketweave No. 1
- 5 Blue Basketweave No. 1
- 6 White Basketweave No. 1
   Background Eggshell Diagonal
      Mosaic No. 1

Yarn Requirements:

Gold—25 yards
Pink—25 yards
Black—16 yards
Yellow—22 yards
Red—14 yards
Blue—20 yards
White—8 yards
Eggshell—125 yards

Plate 22. The Swirl of Butterflies Pillow gains added interest from the use of the Diagonal Mosaic No. 1 for a background stitch. The butterflies have been worked in the Continental No. 1 and Basketweave No. 1.

Birds and Birdhouse Wall Hanging
(12″ by 12″. Fig. 32 and Plate 23)   Executed by Ron Wentz

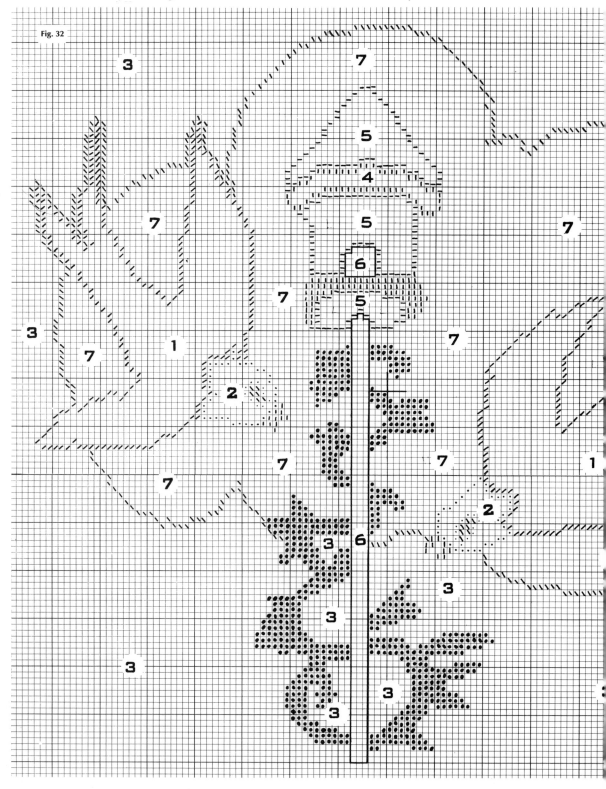

Fig. 32

Colors and Stitches:

/ Pink Continental No. 2
• Red Continental No. 2
\ Turquoise Continental No. 2
| Dark Yellow Continental No. 2
— Light Yellow Continental No. 2
● Dark Green Continental No. 2
1 Pink Basketweave No. 2
2 Red Basketweave No. 2
3 Turquoise Basketweave No. 2
4 Dark Yellow Continental No. 2
5 Light Yellow Basketweave No. 2
6 Brown Basketweave No. 2
7 White Basketweave No. 2

Yarn Requirements:

Pink—25 yards
Red—2 yards
Turquoise—60 yards
Dark Yellow—3 yards
Light Yellow—6 yards
Dark Green—8 yards
Brown—3 yards
White—50 yards

Plate 23. The Birds and Birdhouse Wall Hanging was inspired by an antique gift wrapping. The stitch, Continental No. 2, is excellent for the left-handed needlepointer.

Four Butterflies Pillow

(15" by 15". Fig. 33 and Plate 24)   Executed by Ersi Valavanis

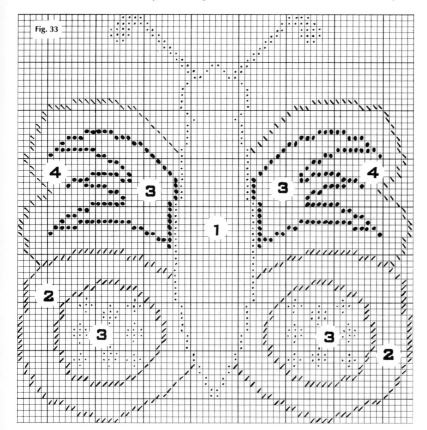

Colors and Stitches:

Work 1 butterfly in each corner.
- • Black Continental No. 1
- / Light Purple Continental No. 1
- \ Blue Continental No. 1
- • Dark Purple Continental No. 1
- 1 Black Basketweave No. 1
- 2 Light Purple Basketweave No. 1
- 3 Dark Purple Basketweave No. 1
- 4 Blue Basketweave No. 1
  Background Gold Basketweave No. 1

Yarn Requirements:

Black—28 yards
Light Purple—24 yards
Dark Purple—40 yards
Blue—40 yards
Gold—100 yards

Plate 24. *The Four Butterflies Pillow is one basic design that has been repeated in each corner of the canvas. This technique can be employed with many small designs where a larger finished needlepoint is required.*

44

Shy Owl Picture

(9″ by 9″. Fig. 34 and Plate 25)   Executed by Ron Wentz

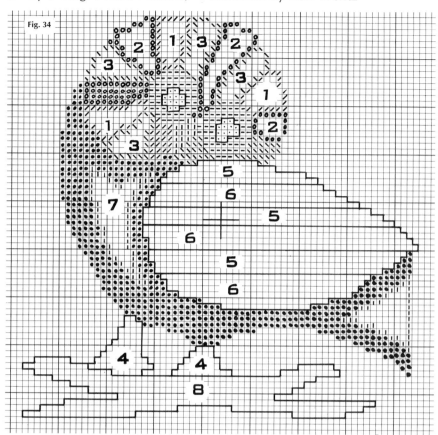

Colors and Stitches:

/ Shocking Pink Continental No. 1
O Dark Pink Continental No. 1
\ Red Continental Stitch No. 1
• Black Continental No. 1
I Gold Continental No. 1
— White Continental No. 1
1 Shocking Pink Continental No. 1
2 Dark Pink Continental No. 1
3 Red Continental No. 1
4 Black Continental No. 1
5 Light Blue Basketweave No. 1
6 Dark Blue Basketweave No. 1
7 Gold Continental No. 1
8 Green Continental No. 1
   Background Eggshell
       Basketweave No. 1

Yarn Requirements:

Shocking Pink—4 yards
Dark Pink—4 yards
Red—5 yards
Black—5 yards
Gold—3 yards
White—5 yards
Light Blue—7 yards
Dark Blue—7 yards
Green—6 yards
Eggshell—45 yards

Plate 25. The Shy Owl Picture would make a welcome addition to any child's room. It could also be used as a pincushion or sachet.

Perky Owl Picture

(9" by 9". Fig. 35 and Plate 26)

Fig. 35

Colors and Stitches:

/ Red Continental No. 1
• Light Pink Continental No. 1
− White Continental No. 1
\ Shocking Pink Continental No. 1
1 Black Continental No. 1
2 Gold Continental No. 1
3 Light Pink Continental No. 1
4 Orange Continental No. 1
   Background Eggshell
     Basketweave No. 1

Yarn Requirements:

Red—16 yards
Light Pink—6 yards
White—¾ yard
Shocking Pink—6 yards
Black—5 yards
Gold—½ yard
Orange—6 yards
Eggshell—50 yards

Plate 26. The Perky Owl Picture is a companion to the Shy Owl Picture. The two designs would be effective if appliquéd to a long pillow or headboard.

Aztec Bird Wall Hanging

(10″ by 10″. Fig. 36 and Plate 27)

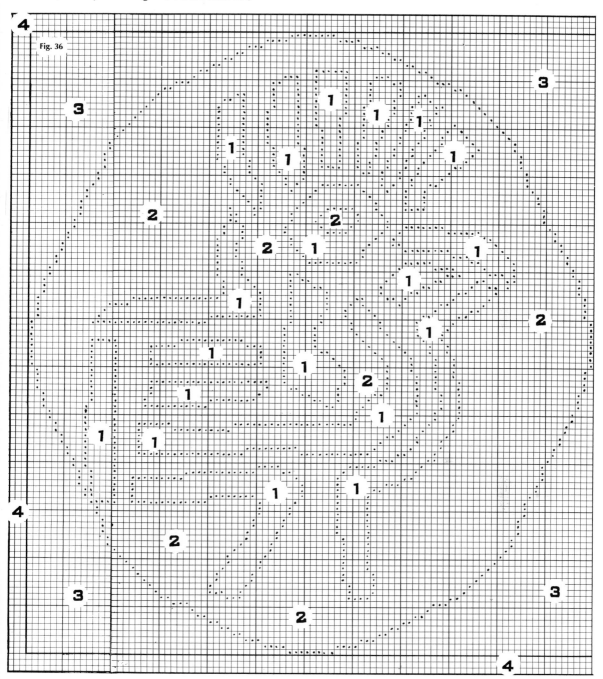

Fig. 36

Colors and Stitches:

- • Rust Continental No. 1
- 1 Rust Basketweave No. 1
- 2 Yellow Diagonal Mosaic No. 1
- 3 Gold and Brown Scotch No. 3
  Alternating
- 4 Rust Slanting Gobelin No. 1 and
  Stem No. 3

Yarn Requirements:

Rust—30 yards
Yellow—35 yards
Gold—20 yards
Brown—20 yards

Plate 27. The Aztec Bird Wall Hanging was inspired by an ancient Aztec stone carving. The background was enlivened by the use of the Diagonal Mosaic No. 1 and the Scotch No. 1 in alternating colors, resulting is a checkerboard effect.

Ladybug Sash

(2½″ wide. Fig. 37 and Plate 28)

Fig. 37

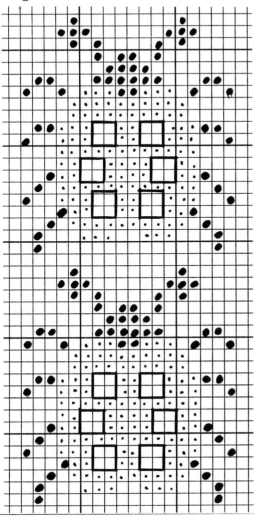

Colors and Stitches:

Work the right side in Stitch No. 2 and the left side in Stitch No. 1

- ● Black Continental No. 1 and Continental No. 2
- • Red Continental No. 1 and Continental No. 2
- □ Black Scotch No. 1 and Scotch No. 2 Background Tan Stem No. 3 and Stem No. 4

Yarn Requirements per Bug:

Red—2 yards
Black—2 yards
Tan—8 yards

Plate 28. The Ladybug Sash would also make a handsome strap for a shoulder or tote bag. Several rows of this design would also be effective if appliquéd to a long, narrow pillow top.

Pennsylvania Dutch Hearts Pillow

(11" by 11". Fig. 38 and Plate 29)

Work the design as charted and then turn the chart upside down to work the other side.

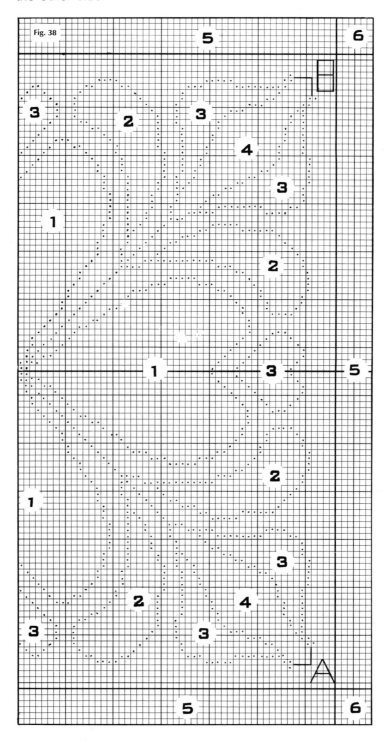

Fig. 38

Colors and Stitches:

A corners are worked in No. 1 stitches and B corners are worked in No. 2 stitches.

- Medium Pink Continental No. 1 and Continental No. 2
1 Red and White Double Cross
2 Dark Purple and Dark Rose Mosiac No. 1 and Mosiac No. 2
3 Shocking Pink Diagonal Mosaic No. 1 and Diagonal Mosaic No. 2
4 Light Lavender Diagonal Mosaic No. 1 and Diagonal Mosaic No. 2
5 Light Lavender and Dark Purple Scotch No. 1 and Scotch No. 2 Alternating
6 Dark Purple Continental No. 1 and Continental No. 2
   Background Light Pink Basketweave No. 1 and Basketweave No. 2

Yarn Requirements:

Medium Pink—15 yards
Red—12 yards
White—10 yards
Dark Purple—12 yards
Dark Rose—10 yards
Shocking Pink—14 yards
Light Lavender—10 yards
Light Pink—20 yards

Plate 29. The Pennsylvania Dutch Hearts Pillow has a variety of needlepoint stitches, all worked in different directions and resulting in a perfectly symmetrical design. The stitches are Basketweave No. 1 and No. 2, Mosaic No. 1 and No. 2, Diagonal Mosaic No. 1 and No. 2, and Double Cross.

Four Flowers Pillow

(15″ by 15″. Fig. 39 and Plate 30)   Executed by Ersi Valavanis

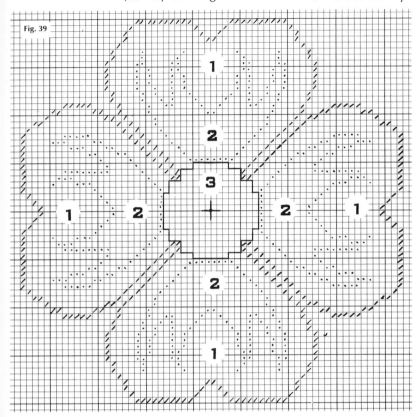

Fig. 39

Colors and Stitches:

Flower Petals—Work 2 flowers in opposite corners in the colors and stitches charted. Work the other 2 flowers in the other corners in reversed colors.

/ Bright Rose Continental No. 1
• Dark Purple Continental No. 1
1 Bright Rose
   Basketweave No. 1
2 Dark Purple
   Basketweave No. 1
Flower Centers—
   3 Light Purple and Pink French Knots Mixed
   Background Olive Basketweave No. 1

Yarn Requirements:

Bright Rose—40 yards
Light Purple—40 yards
Pink—40 yards
Dark Purple—40 yards
Olive—75 yards

Plate 30. The Four Flowers Pillow is an example of canvas embroidery. The center of each flower is filled with French Knots, an embroidery stitch, for added texture.

Tulips Eyeglass Case or Checkbook Cover

(6¾'' by 3½''. Fig. 40 and Plate 31)

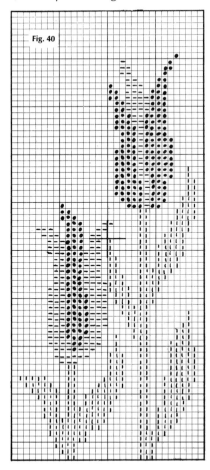

Fig. 40

Colors and Stitches:

- ● Light Pink Continental No. 1
- ─ Dark Pink Continental No. 1
- I Green Continental No. 1
  Background Blue
    Basketweave No. 1

Yarn Requirements for One Side:

Light Pink—3 yards
Dark Pink—3 yards
Green—5 yards
Blue—13 yards

Plate 31. The Tulips Eyeglass Case or Checkbook Cover is a stylized design of the popular harbinger of spring. It can be worked in many color combinations.

Tulip Belt

(2⅜" wide. Fig. 41 and Plate 32)

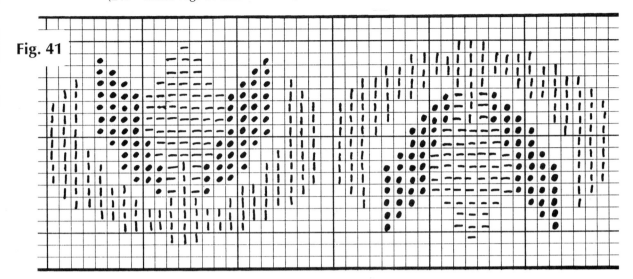

Fig. 41

Colors and Stitches:

  — Light Shade of any color Continental No. 1

  ● Dark Shade of the same color Continental No. 1

  I Dark Green Continental No. 1
    Background Light Green
    Basketweave No. 1

Yarn Requirements per Flower:

Light Shade—¾ yard
Dark Shade—1 yard
Dark Green—1½ yards
Light Green—3 yards

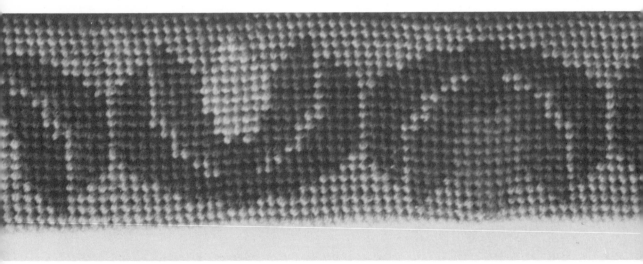

Plate 32. The Tulip Belt shows one basic design which has been reversed for added interest. Each tulip flower has been worked in two shades of the same color. Small scraps of yarn could be used for a bright, cheerful belt.

Strawberries and Flowers Pillow
(8½″ by 10″. Fig. 42 and Plate 33)

Colors and Stitches:

/ Shocking Pink Continental No. 1
● Light Pink Continental No. 1
• Olive Continental No. 1
+ Black French Knots
1 Gold Vertical Satin
2 Light Pink Vertical Satin
3 Dark Pink Vertical Satin
  Background Eggshell
    Continental No. 1

Yarn Requirements per Flower or Strawberry:

Shocking Pink—2 yards
Light Pink—3 yards
Dark Pink—1½ yards
Olive—1 yard
Black—1 yard
Gold—¾ yard
Eggshell—10 yards

Plate 33. The Strawberries and Flowers Pillow incorporates two embroidery stitches, the Satin and French Knot, for added dimension. The design can be continued at will for any size product from small pillow to large rug.

Circle of Flowers Pillow
(15″ by 15″. Fig. 43 and Plate 34)

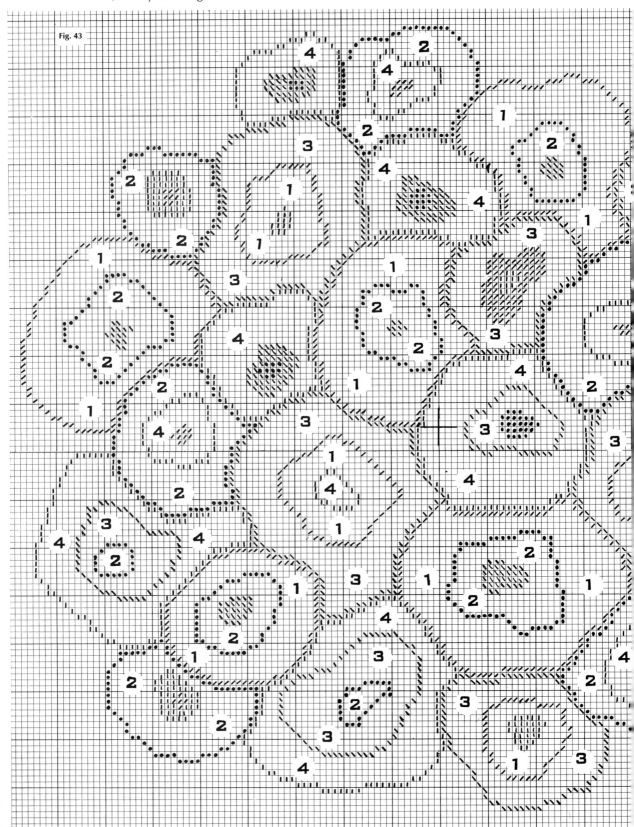

Fig. 43

Colors and Stitches:

/ Light Blue Continental No. 1
● Gold Continental No. 1
\ Pink Continental No. 1
| Yellow Continental No. 1
1 Light Blue Basketweave No. 1
2 Gold Basketweave No. 1
3 Pink Basketweave No. 1
4 Yellow Basketweave No. 1
  Background Eggshell Scotch No. 1

Yarn Requirements:

Light Blue—45 yards
Gold—47 yards
Pink—43 yards
Yellow—44 yards
Eggshell—46 yards

Plate 34. The Circle of Flowers Pillow is a study in pastels. The flat texture of the stitch used for the flowers is accented by the bold Scotch No. 1 stitch used for the background.

Anemones Pillow and Wall Hanging

(13″ by 13″. Fig. 44 and Plates 35 and 36)
Wall Hanging Executed by Millie Wadler

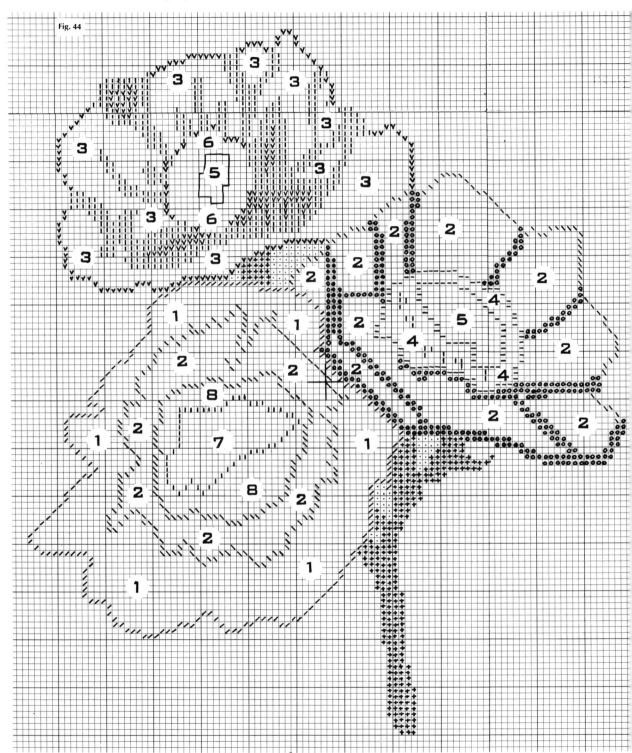

Fig. 44

Colors and Stitches:

/ Medium Rose Continental No. 1
\ Dark Rose Continental No. 1
I Dark Purple Continental No. 1
V Light Purple Continental No. 1
— White Continental No. 1
+ Medium Olive Continental No. 1
• Eggshell Continental No. 1
1 Medium Rose Basketweave No. 1
2 Dark Rose Basketweave No. 1
3 Light Purple Basketweave No. 1
4 White Basketweave No. 1
5 Dark Purple French Knots
6 White Radiating Satin
7 Dark Purple Basketweave No. 1
8 White and Dark Purple French Knots
   Mixed
   Background Eggshell
    Basketweave No. 1

Yarn Requirements:

Medium Rose—30 yards
Dark Rose—30 yards
Dark Purple—30 yards
Light Purple—32 yards
White—4 yards
Medium Olive—5 yards
Eggshell—36 yards

Plate 35. The Anemones Pillow has a textured center of French Knots and Satin Stitch. These embroidery stitches contrast effectively with the flat surface of the Continental No. 1 and Basketweave No. 1.

Plate 36. The Anemones Wall Hanging is basically the same design as the Anemones Pillow except that it has been worked entirely in the Continental No. 1 and Basketweave No. 1. This completely flat surface lends itself more effectively to a picture treatment.

Splash of Flowers Pillow
(15" by 15". Fig. 45 and Plate 37)

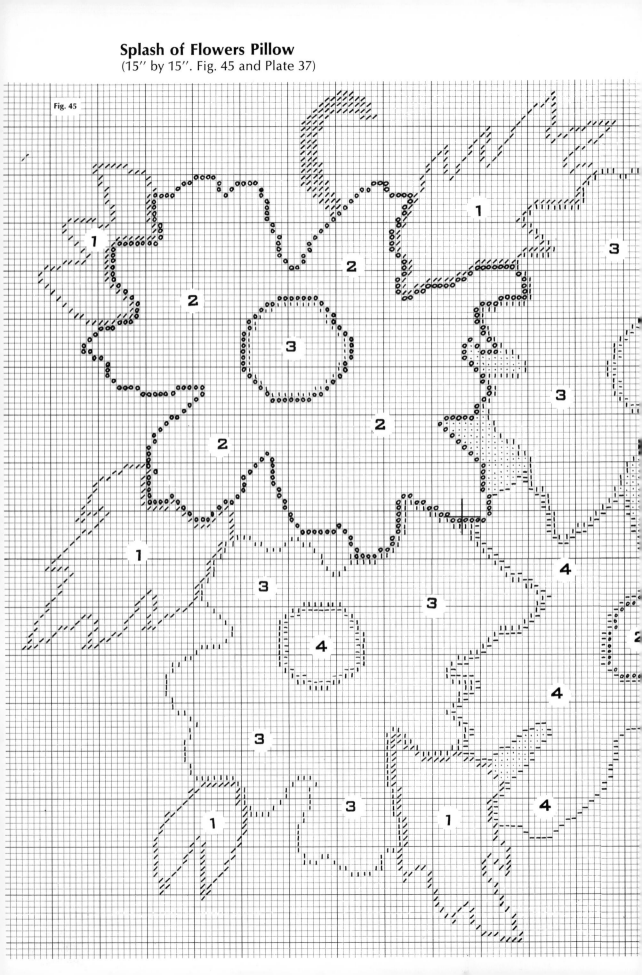

Colors and Stitches:

/ Olive Continental No. 1
O Light Rose Continental No. 1
I Blue Continental No. 1
− Dark Rose Continental No. 1
• Eggshell Diagonal Mosaic No. 1
1 Olive Basketweave No. 1
2 Light Rose Basketweave No. 1
3 Blue Basketweave No. 1
4 Dark Rose Basketweave No. 1
  Background Eggshell
      Diagonal Mosaic No. 1

Yarn Requirements:

Olive—20 yards
Light Rose—48 yards
Blue—64 yards
Dark Rose—52 yards
Eggshell—50 yards

Plate 37. The Splash of Flowers Pillow gains its impact from its use of large areas of color in the design. Note that the background has been kept to a minimum.

Flower with Tendrils Pillow

(8″ by 8″. Fig. 46 and Plate 38)

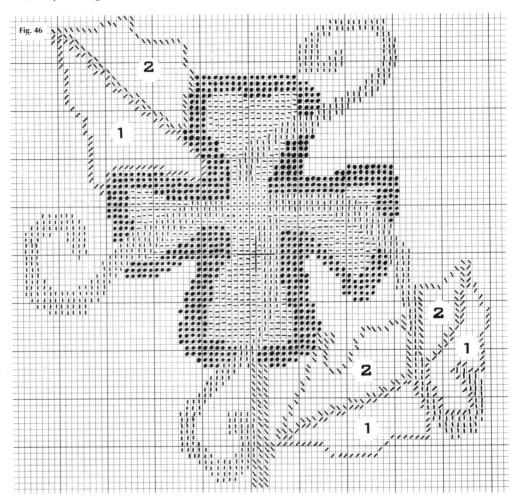

Fig. 46

Colors and Stitches:

- ╱ Dark Green Continental No. 1
- ╲ Light Green Continental No. 1
- ● Gold Continental No. 1
- | Yellow Continental No. 2
- • Brown Continental No. 1
- – Orange Continental No. 1
- 1 Dark Green
     Basketweave No. 1
- 2 Light Green
     Basketweave No. 1
   Background Light Brown
     Basketweave No. 1

Yarn Requirements:

Dark Green—6 yards
Light Green—6 yards
Gold—10 yards
Yellow—6 yards
Brown—½ yard
Orange—4 yards
Light Brown—40 yards

Plate 38. The Flower with Tendrils Pillow effectively combines the Continental No. 1 with the Continental No. 2 stitch. The long tendrils were worked in the Continental No. 2 to contrast with the rest of the design stitch.

Trellis of Roses Pillow

(12" by 12". Fig. 47 and Plate 39)   Executed by Rena Sherman

Plate 39. The Trellis of Roses Pillow is worked in shades of pink. It could also be effectively worked in shades of yellow, gold, rust, or red, depending upon the decorating scheme involved.

Colors and Stitches:

/ Dark Pink Continental No. 1
\ Medium Pink Continental No. 1
I Light Pink Continental No. 1
− Dark Green Continental No. 1
• Light Green Continental No. 1
1 Dark Pink Basketweave No. 1
2 Medium Pink Basketweave No. 1
3 Light Pink Basketweave No. 1
4 Dark Green Basketweave No. 1
5 Light Green Basketweave No. 1
 Work black diagonal lines in background every 1½" apart to form the trellis pattern using Continental No. 1
 Background Eggshell Basketweave No. 1

Yarn Requirements:

Dark Pink—20 yards
Medium Pink—20 yards
Light Pink—20 yards
Dark Green—10 yards
Light Green—10 yards
Black—12 yards
Eggshell—50 yards

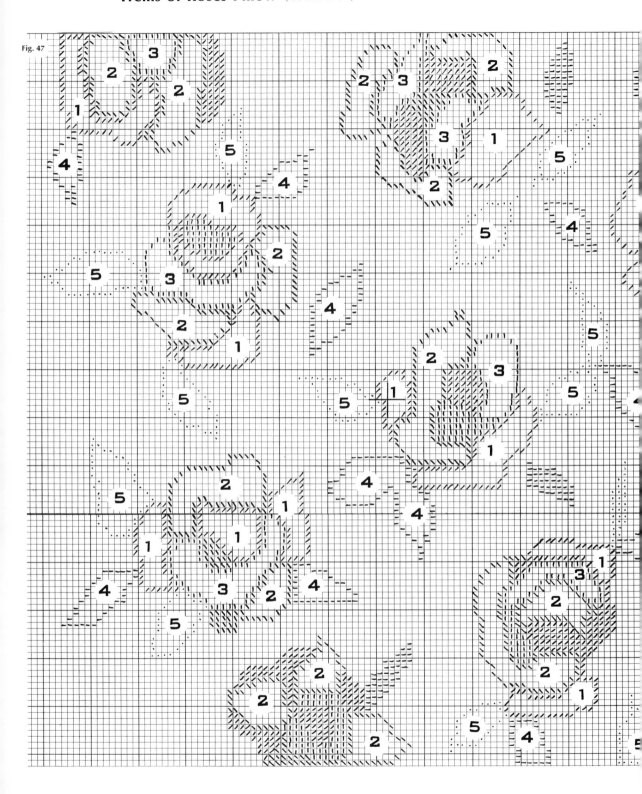

Fig. 47

Impressionistic Flowers Pillow
(17″ by 17″. Fig. 48 and Plate 40)

Plate 40. The Impressionistic Flowers Pillow was adapted from an upholstery fabric. In many cases the fabric used in upholstery or draperies can serve as the inspiration for a needlepoint accessory.

Colors and Stitches:

⁄ Blue Continental No. 1
Ι Yellow Continental No. 1
⧹ Pink Continental No. 1
− Red Continental No. 1
• Orange Continental No. 1
○ Purple Continental No. 1
● Green Continental No. 1
1 Blue Basketweave No. 1
2 Yellow Basketweave No. 1
3 Pink Basketweave No. 1
4 Red Basketweave No. 1
5 Orange Basketweave No. 1
6 Purple Basketweave No. 1
7 Green Basketweave No. 1
   Background Eggshell
     Basketweave No. 1

Yarn Requirements:

Blue—14 yards
Yellow—18 yards
Pink—44 yards
Red—14 yards
Orange—24 yards
Purple—12 yards
Green—10 yards
Eggshell—120 yards

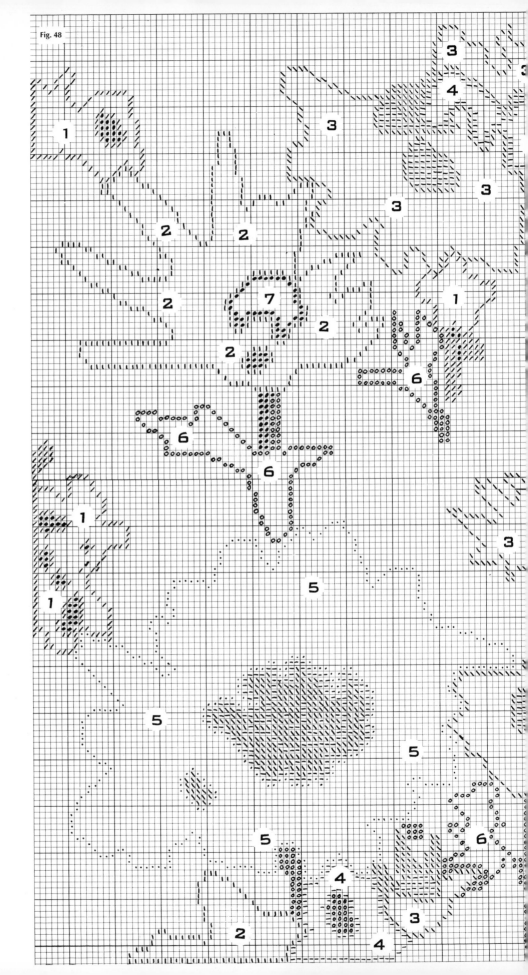

Fig. 48

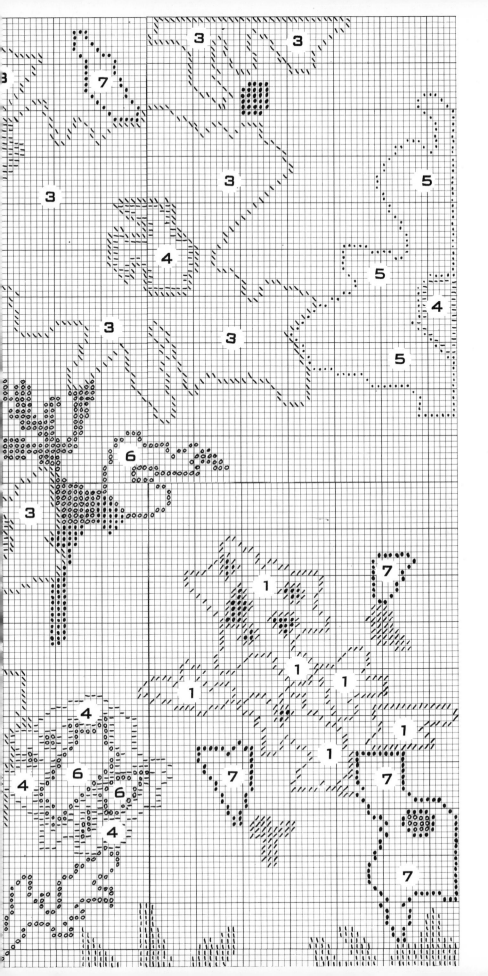

Hearts and Ribbon Pillow
(10″ by 10″. Fig. 49 and Plate 41)　Executed by Rena Sherman

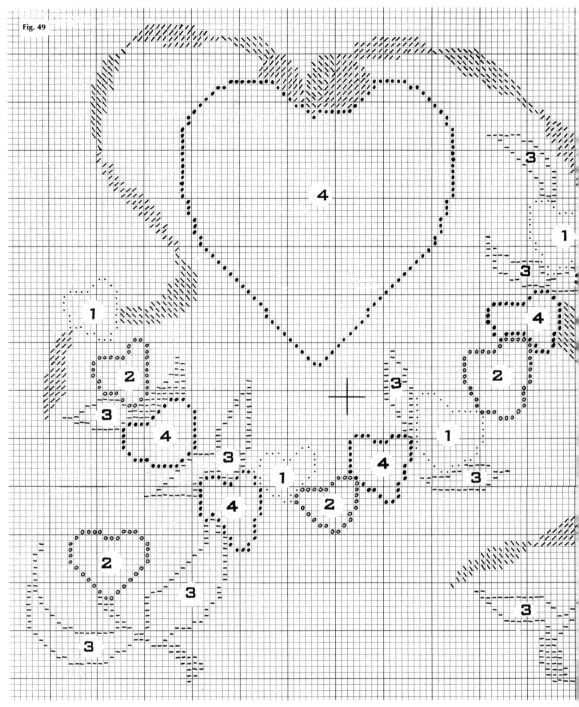

Fig. 49

Colors and Stitches:

/ Light Blue Continental No. 1
\ Dark Blue Continental No. 1
• Light Pink Continental No. 1
○ Dark Pink Continental No. 1
– Green Continental No. 1
● Red Continental No. 1
1 Light Pink Basketweave No. 1
2 Dark Pink Basketweave No. 1
3 Green Basketweave No. 1
4 Red Basketweave No. 1
  Background Light Tan
    Basketweave No. 1

Yarn Requirements:

Light Blue—4 yards
Dark Blue—5 yards
Light Pink—3 yards
Dark Pink—5 yards
Green—10 yards
Red—16 yards
Light Tan—60 yards

Plate 41. The Hearts and Ribbon Pillow would make an excellent Valentine remembrance, either as a pillow or the top of a box to contain those special letters.

Flowers on Checkered Background Pillow

(13″ by 13″. Fig. 50 and Plate 42)

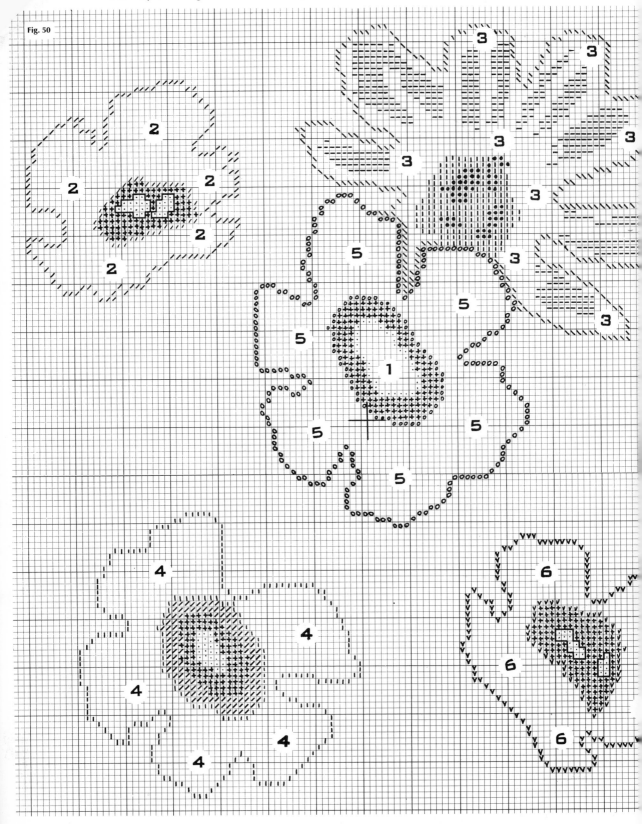

Fig. 50

Colors and Stitches:

- • Purple Continental No. 1
- / Orange Continental No. 1
- + Light Gray/Green
    Continental No. 1
- \ Turquoise Continental No. 1
- • Red Continental No. 1
- I Medium Pink Continental No. 1
- − White Continental No. 1
- O Yellow Continental No. 1
- V Rose Continental No. 1
- 1 Purple Basketweave No. 1
- 2 Orange Basketweave No. 1
- 3 Turquoise Basketweave No. 1
- 4 Medium Pink Basketweave No. 1
- 5 Yellow Basketweave No. 1
- 6 Rose Basketweave No. 1

    Background: Work every 10th row with 1 row of White Continental No. 2. Fill in the squares with Light, Medium, and Dark Green Continental No. 1.

Yarn Requirements:

Purple—2 yards
Orange—10 yards
Light Gray/Green—8 yards
Turquoise—8 yards
Red—1 yard
Medium Pink—10 yards
White—20 yards
Yellow—12 yards
Rose—10 yards
Light Green—30 yards
Medium Green—30 yards
Dark Green—30 yards

Plate 42. The Flowers on Checkered Background Pillow is worked on various shades of green background. The background color could also be various shades of colors used in your decorating scheme.

Zebra and Flowers Pillow
(13½″ by 13½″. Fig. 51 and Plate 43) Executed by Rena Sherman

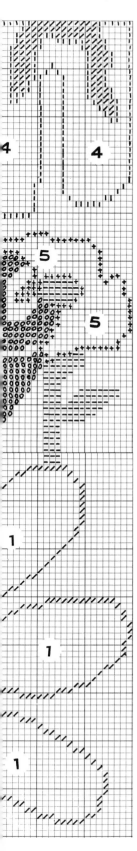

Colors and Stitches:

/ Yellow Continental No. 1
\ Dark Orange Continental No. 1
• Light Orange Continental No. 1
– Olive Continental No. 1
I Violet Continental No. 1
O Black Continental No. 1
+ Blue Continental No. 1
1 Yellow Basketweave No. 1
2 Light Orange Basketweave No. 1
3 Olive Basketweave No. 1
4 Violet Basketweave No. 1
5 Blue Basketweave No. 1
Background Eggshell
    Basketweave No. 1

Yarn Requirements:

Yellow—25 yards
Dark Orange—12 yards
Light Orange—14 yards
Olive—8 yards
Violet—16 yards
Black—20 yards
Blue—8 yards
Eggshell—85 yards

Plate 43. The Zebra and Flowers Pillow would be equally effective in a contemporary or traditional setting. Vary the colors of the flowers to match or contrast with the colors in your room.

Hearts Sash

(2¼" wide. Fig. 52 and Plate 44)

Fig. 52

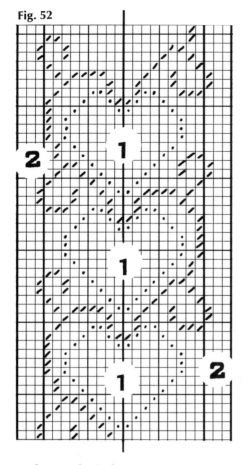

Colors and Stitches:

Stitches on the left side are No. 2 and the stitches on the right side are No. 1.

- • Red Continental No. 1 and Continental No. 2
- ⁄ Dark Pink Continental No. 1 and Continental No. 2
- 1 Fill each heart with parallel rows of Dark Purple, Light Purple, Dark Pink, and Dark Purple Continental No. 1 and Continental No. 2
- 2 Dark Purple Stem No. 3 and Stem No. 4.

Background Light Pink Continental No. 1 and Continental No. 2

Yarn Requirements per Heart:

Red—1 yard
Dark Pink—4 yards
Dark Purple—3 yards
Light Purple—¾ yard
Light Pink—5 yards

74

Plate 44. The Hearts Sash would also make an effective design for a pair of suspenders. The design could be worked in shades of almost any color to suit your fancy.

Tulip Flower Wall Hanging

(9" by 9". Fig. 53 and Plate 45)

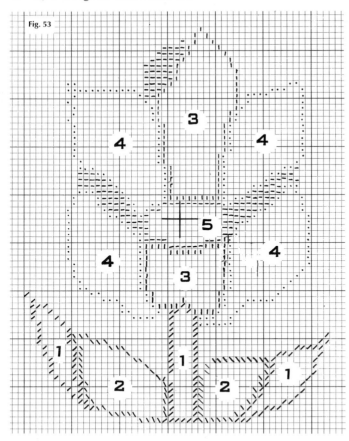

Fig. 53

Colors and Stitches:

/ Dark Green Continental No. 1
\ Light Green Continental No. 1
| Purple Continental No. 1
− Yellow Continental No. 1
• Red Continental No. 1
1 Dark Green Basketweave No. 1
2 Light Green Basketweave No. 1
3 Purple Basketweave No. 1
4 Red Basketweave No. 1
5 Yellow Basketweave No. 1
Background Light Brown
Basketweave No. 1

Yarn Requirements:

Dark Green—6 yards
Light Green—5 yards
Purple—6 yards
Yellow—6 yards
Red—9 yards
Light Brown—50 yards

Small Flower Wall Hanging

(9'' by 9''. Fig. 54 and Plate 45)

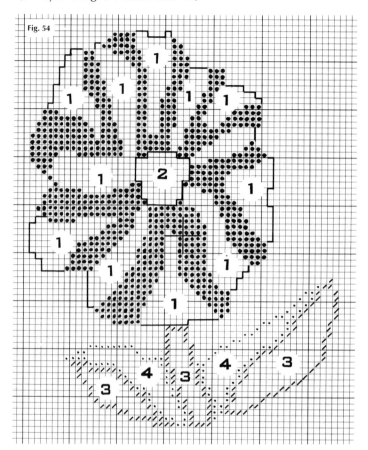

Fig. 54

Colors and Stitches:

- Dark Rose Continental No. 1
- / Light Green Continental No. 1
- · Dark Green Continental No. 1
- 1 Light Rose Basketweave No. 1
- 2 Yellow Baasketweave No. 1
- 3 Light Green Basketweave No. 1
- 4 Dark Green Basketweave No. 1
  Background Light Brown
    Basketweave No.1

Yarn Requirements:

Dark Rose—12 yards
Light Green—5 yards
Dark Green—4 yards
Light Rose—12 yards
Yellow—1 yard
Light Brown—50 yards

Plate 45. The Tulip Flower (bottom) and Small Flower (top) canvases are appliqué mounted to a felt-covered background board. The edges of the canvas are trimmed with a bright fabric braid and small pompoms at the corners provide added interest.

Bouquet of Flowers Pillow
(15" by 15". Fig. 55 and Plate 46)

Fig. 55

Colors and Stitches:

- • Dark Pink Continental No. 1
- ○ Brown Continental No. 1
- \ Gray Continental No. 1
- / Green Continental No. 1
- 1 Dark Rose Basketweave No. 1
- 2 Red Basketweave No. 1
- 3 Light Gold Basketweave No. 1
- 4 Dark Gold Basketweave No. 1
- 5 Light Pink Basketweave No. 1
- 6 Dark Pink Basketweave No. 1
- 7 Light Blue Basketweave No. 1
- 8 Dark Blue Basketweave No. 1
- 9 Black Basketweave No. 1
  Background Eggshell
    Basketweave No.1

Yarn Requirements:

Dark Pink—10 yards
Brown—4 yards
Gray—4 yards
Green—10 yards
Dark Rose—12 yards
Red—10 yards
Light Gold—12 yards
Dark Gold—10 yards
Light Pink—12 yards
Light Blue—12 yards
Dark Blue—10 yards
Black—4 yards
Eggshell—90 yards

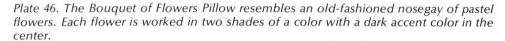

Plate 46. The Bouquet of Flowers Pillow resembles an old-fashioned nosegay of pastel flowers. Each flower is worked in two shades of a color with a dark accent color in the center.

Three Carnations Pillow
(12″ by 12″. Fig. 56 and Plate 47)

Fig. 56

Colors and Stitches:

| Light Green Continental No. 1
● Dark Green Continental No. 1
• Light Green Diagonal
    Mosaic No. 1
╱ Light Pink Diagonal
    Mosaic No. 1
╲ Medium Pink Diagonal
    Mosaic No. 1
— Dark Pink Diagonal
    Mosaic No. 1
1 Light Pink Diagonal
    Mosaic No. 1
2 Dark Pink Diagonal
    Mosaic No. 1
3 Medium Pink Diagonal
    Mosaic No. 1
4 Dark Pink Diagonal
    Mosaic No. 1
    Background Eggshell
    Basketweave No. 1

Yarn Requirements:

Light Green—14 yards
Dark Green—18 yards
Light Pink—8 yards
Medium Pink—12 yards
Dark Pink—8 yards
Eggshell—90 yards

Plate 47. The Three Carnations Pillow was inspired by an old piano shawl which had large carnations embroidered with chenille. The design has been worked with the Diagonal Mosaic No. 1 against a flat background of Basketweave No. 1.

Sunflower Pillow
(15″ by 15″. Fig. 57 and Plate 48)   Executed by Ron Wentz

Fig. 57

Colors and Stitches:

- • Light Gold Continental No. 1
- I Dark Gold Continental No. 1
- / Brown Continental No. 1
- − Black French Knots
- 1 Light Gold Scotch No. 1
- 2 Dark Gold Scotch No. 1
- 3 Brown French Knots
  Background Eggshell
  Basketweave No. 1

Yarn Requirements:

Light Gold—60 yards
Dark Gold—60 yards
Brown—20 yards
Black—8 yards
Eggshell—90 yards

Plate 48. The Sunflower Pillow is a bold design worked with equally bold stitches. The petals are worked with Scotch No. 1 and the center is filled with a massive cluster of French Knots. Notice that all the Scotch No. 1 stitches line up with one another.

Smiling Flower Wall Hanging

(7″ by 7″. Fig. 58 and Plate 49)

Fig. 58

Colors and Stitches:

| Black Continental No. 1
● Orange Continental No. 1
／ Olive Continental No. 1
1 Yellow Basketweave No. 1
2 Pink Basketweave No. 1
   Background Eggshell
      Diagonal Mosaic No. 1

Yarn Requirements:

Black—¾ yard
Orange—12 yards
Olive—1 yard
Yellow—12 yards
Pink—2 yards
Eggshell—30 yards

Plate 49. The Smiling Flower Wall Hanging is a charming adaptation of the smiling face that has been adorning so many items of late. The flat design stitches contrast effectively with the texture of the Diagonal Mosaic No. 1 background stitch.

Pierced Heart Pincushion or Sachet

(4½'' by 4½''. Fig. 59 and Plate 50)

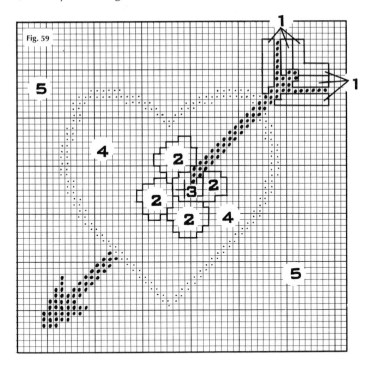

Fig. 59

Colors and Stitches:

- • Red Continental No. 1
- ● Dark Gold Continental No. 1
- 1 Light Gold Stem No. 1 and Slanting Gobelin No. 4
- 2 Dark Purple Diagonal Satin
- 3 Light Yellow French Knots
- 4 Light and Dark Pink Alternating Diagonal Mosaic No. 1
- 5 Light Yellow and Dark Yellow Alternating Stem No. 3

Yarn Requirements:

Red—3 yards
Light Pink—4 yards
Dark Pink—4 yards
Dark Purple—2 yards
Light Gold—1½ yards
Dark Gold—2½ yards
Light Yellow—6 yards
Dark Yellow—6 yards

Tulip Coaster, Pincushion, or Sachet

(4″ by 4″. Fig. 60 and Plate 50)

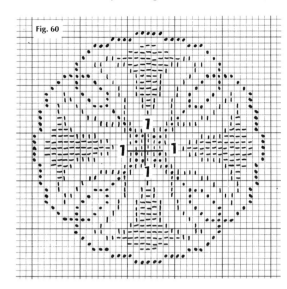

Fig. 60

Colors and Stitches:

- ● Orange Continental No. 1
- − Light Rust Continental No. 1
- I Dark Rust Continental No. 1
- 1 Dark Rust Continental No. 1
  Background Brown Continental No. 1
  or Scotch No. 1
  Border of Pincushion or Sachet—
  Stem No. 3 and Slanting Gobelin
  No. 1

Yarn Requirements:

Orange—4 yards
Light Rust—4 yards
Dark Rust—4 yards
Brown—6 yards

Plate 50. *The Pierced Heart Pincushion or sachet* (right) *is a study in effective use of decorative stitches. Only 4½″ square, it contains seven stitches: Continental No. 1, Stem No. 1 and No. 3, Slanting Gobelin No. 4, Diagonal Satin, French Knots, and Diagonal Mosaic No. 1. The Tulip Pincushion or Sachet design* (left) *has also been used as a coaster* (center).

Basket of Strawberries Wall Hanging
(9" by 9". Fig. 61 and Plate 51)

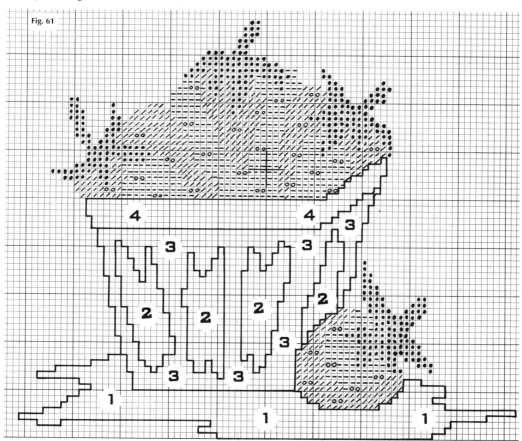

Colors and Stitches:

/ Dark Red Continental No. 1
− Light Red Continental No. 1
○ Black Continental No. 1
● Green Continental No. 1
1 Gray Basketweave No. 1
2 Light Brown Basketweave No. 1
3 Dark Brown Basketweave No. 1
4 Light Brown Diagonal
    Mosaic No. 1
  Background Eggshell
  Scotch No. 1

Yarn Requirements:

Dark Red—5 yards
Light Red—5 yards
Black—1 yard
Green—4 yards
Gray—5 yards
Light Brown—6 yards
Dark Brown—4 yards
Eggshell—55 yards

Plate 51. Basket of Strawberries Wall Hanging is worked with Continental No. 1, Basketweave No. 1, Diagonal Mosaic No. 1, and Scotch No. 1.

Basket of Cherries Wall Hanging
(9″ by 9″. Fig. 62 and Plate 52)

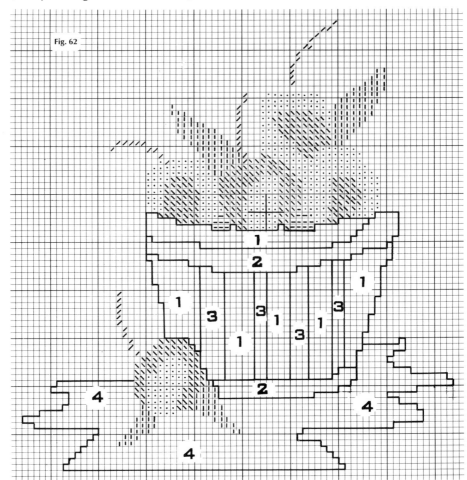

Fig. 62

Colors and Stitches:

/ Dark Green Continental No. 2
• Dark Red Continental No. 1
\ Light Red Continental No. 1
− Black Continental No. 2
1 Light Brown Basketweave No. 2
2 Medium Brown
    Basketweave No. 2
3 Dark Brown Basketweave No. 2
4 Gray Basketweave No. 2
   Background Eggshell
     Mosaic No. 2

Yarn Requirements:

Dark Green—2 yards
Dark Red—5 yards
Light Red—5 yards
Black—½ yard
Light Green—3 yards
Light Brown—6 yards
Medium Brown—3 yards
Dark Brown—1 yard
Gray—5 yards
Eggshell—55 yards

Plate 52. Basket of Cherries Wall Hanging is an ideal proje
for the left-handed needlepointer. It is worked with Co
tinental No. 2, Basketweave No. 2, and Mosaic No. 2.

Mushroom Coaster

(3½" by 3½". Fig. 63 and Plate 53)

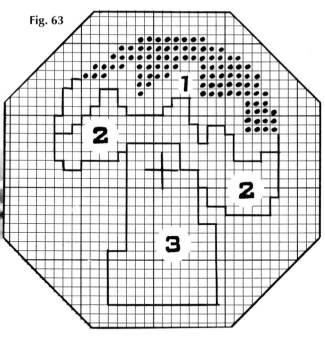

Fig. 63

Colors and Stitches:

- Blue Continental No. 1
- 1 Red Vertical Satin
- 2 Purple Diagonal Mosaic No. 1
- 3 Brown Cashmere No. 1
  Background Rows of Gold and Yellow Continental No. 1 and Basketweave No. 1 alternating

Yarn Requirements:

Blue—1½ yards
Red—2 yards
Purple—2½ yards
Brown—1½ yards
Gold—6 yards
Yellow—6 yards

Plate 53. The Mushroom Coaster, small though it is, is worked with five needlepoint stitches: Continental No. 1, Basketweave No. 1, Cashmere No. 1, Diagonal Mosaic No. 1, and Vertical Satin.

Cherries Eyeglass Case or Checkbook Cover

(6¾" by 3½". Fig. 64 and Plate 54)

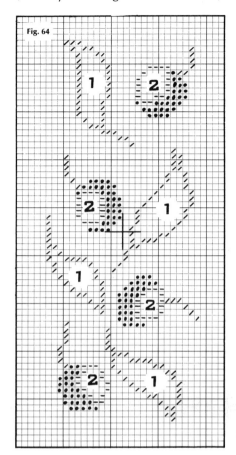

Colors and Stitches:

/ Green Continental No. 1
● Dark Red Continental No. 1
– Light Red Continental No. 1
1 Green Continental No. 1
2 Light Red Continental No. 1
   Background Black
      Basketweave No. 1

Yarn Requirements for One Side:

Green—5 yards
Dark Red—4 yards
Light Red—4 yards
Black—12 yards

Plate 54. The Cherries Eyeglass Case or Check-book Cover design would also be appropriate if expanded to form a pillow or box top.

Fat Mushroom Tote Bag

(9″ by 7½″. Fig. 65 and Plate 55)

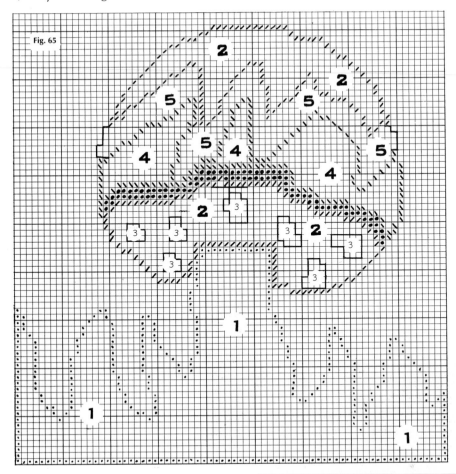

Fig. 65

Colors and Stitches:

- • Green Continental No. 1
- ╱ Dark Blue Continental No. 1
- ● Dark Purple Continental No. 1
- ╲ Light Purple Continental No. 1
- 1 Green Basketweave No. 1
- 2 Dark Blue Basketweave No. 1
- 3 Pink French Knots
- 4 Light Purple Basketweave No. 1
- 5 Red Vertical Satin
   Background Basketweave No. 1

Yarn Requirements:

Green—12 yards
Dark Blue—10 yards
Light Purple—10 yards
Pink—8 yards
Red—6 yards
Gold—25 yards

Plate 55. The Fat Mushroom Tote Bag canvas has been appliquéd to the face of a canvas tote bag. The design incorporates a Vertical Satin Stitch and French Knots for added textural interest.

91

Sliced Mushroom Wall Hanging

(9" by 9". Fig. 66 and Plate 56)

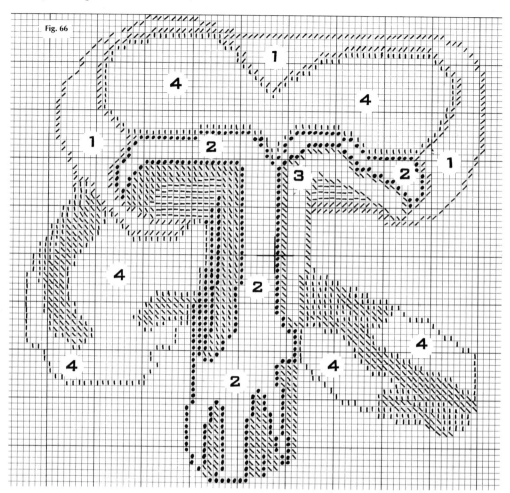

Fig. 66

Colors and Stitches:

/ Eggshell Continental No. 1
● Gray Continental No. 1
\ Dark Brown Continental No. 1
| Light Brown Continental No. 1
1 Eggshell Basketweave No. 1
2 Gray Basketweave No. 1
3 Dark Brown
 Basketweave No. 1
4 Light Brown
 Basketweave No. 1
 Background Olive
 Mosaic No. 1

Yarn Requirements:

Eggshell—6 yards
Gray—7 yards
Dark Brown—9 yards
Light Brown—13 yards
Olive—55 yards

Plate 56. The Sliced Mushroom Wall Hanging is one of a group of four designs that are particularly suited for use in the kitchen. This design, and the next three, gain added interest from the use of textured background stitches.

Sliced Lemon Wall Hanging

(9″ by 9″. Fig. 67 and Plate 57)

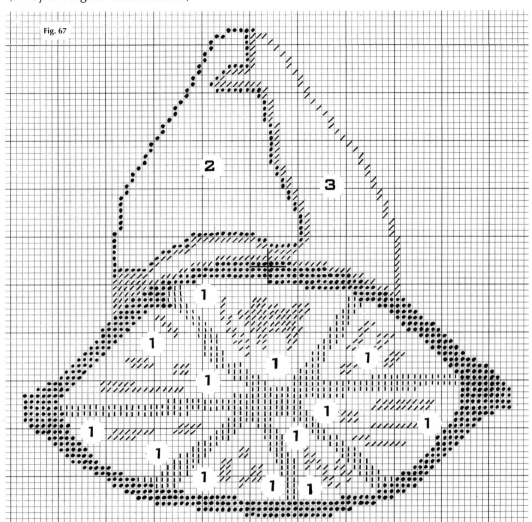

Fig. 67

Colors and Stitches:

I White Continental No. 1
● Dark Yellow
    Continental No. 1
╱ Light Orange
    Continental No. 1
1 Light Yellow
    Continental No. 1
2 Dark Yellow
    Continental No. 1
3 Light Orange
    Continental No. 1
    Background Eggshell
    Diagonal Mosaic No. 1

Yarn Requirements:

White—4 yards
Dark Yellow—10 yards
Light Orange—10 yards
Light Yellow—10 yards
Eggshell—55 yards

Plate 57. The Sliced Lemon Wall Hanging design has been worked with Continental No. 1 and Basketweave No. 1 with the background worked with Diagonal Mosaic No. 1.

Sliced Avocado Wall Hanging

(9" by 9". Fig. 68 and Plate 58)

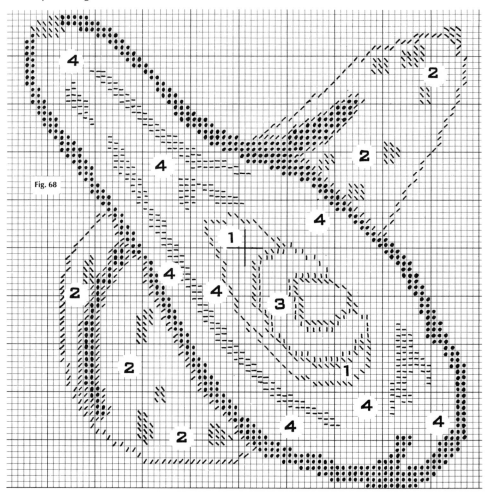

Fig. 68

Colors and Stitches:

\ Dark Brown
　Continental No. 2
● Medium Avocado
　Continental No. 2
/ Dark Avocado
　Continental No. 1
– Eggshell Continental No. 1
| Light Brown
　Continental No. 1
1 Dark Brown
　Continental No. 2
2 Dark Avocado
　Continental No. 1
3 Light Brown
　Continental No. 1
4 Light Avocado
　Continental No. 1
　Background Eggshell
　Mosaic No. 1

Plate 58. The Sliced Avocado Wall Hanging background is worked with Diagonal Mosaic No. 1. The design is worked with Continental No. 1, Continental No. 2, and Basketweave No. 1.

Yarn Requirements:

Dark Brown—3 yards
Medium Avocado—8 yards
Dark Avocado—11 yards
Eggshell—55 yards
Light Brown—1½ yards
Light Avocado—11 yards

Sliced Apple Wall Hanging

(9″ by 9″. Fig. 69 and Plate 59)

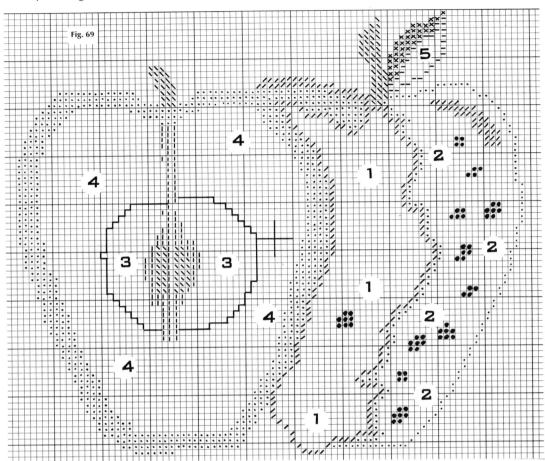

Fig. 69

Colors and Stitches:

- • Pink Continental No. 1
- ╱ Dark Red Continental No. 1
- ● Black Continental No. 1
- ╲ Brown Continental No. 1
- | Yellow Continental No. 1
- − Dark Green
    Continental No. 1
- × Light Green
    Continental No. 1
- 1 Dark Red Basketweave No. 1
- 2 Pink Basketweave No. 1
- 3 Eggshell Basketweave No. 1
- 4 White Diagonal Mosaic No. 1
- 5 Dark Green
    Basketweave No. 1
- Background Olive Diagonal
    Mosaic No. 1

Yarn Requirements:

Pink—15 yards
Dark Red—12 yards
Black—1 yard
Brown—1 yard
Yellow—1 yard
Dark Green—½ yard
Light Green—½ yard
Eggshell—2½ yards
White—7 yards
Olive—50 yards

Plate 59. The Sliced Apple Wall Hanging has a portion of the design worked with Diagonal Mosaic No. 1. The background is also worked with Diagonal Mosaic No. 1.

Three Mushrooms Tote Bag

(9″ by 9″. Fig. 70 and Plate 60)   Executed by Ron Wentz

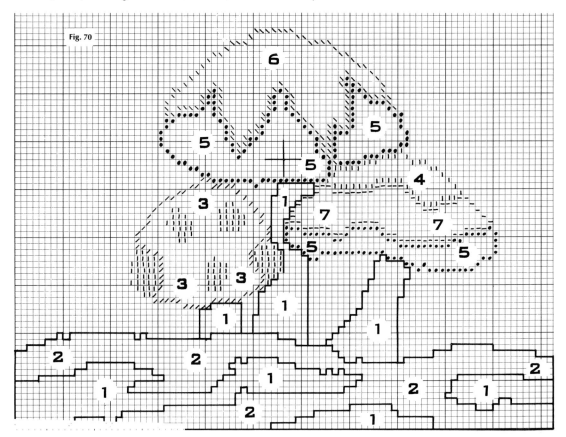

Fig. 70

Colors and Stitches:

/ Orange Continental No. 1
| Red Continental No. 1
● Dark Rose Continental No. 1
\ Purple Continental No. 1
− Yellow Continental No. 1
1 Light Green Basketweave No. 1
2 Dark Green Basketweave No.
3 Orange Basketweave No. 1
4 Red Basketweave No. 1
5 Dark Rose Basketweave No. 1
6 Purple Basketweave No. 1
7 Yellow Basketweave No. 1
  Background Eggshell
    Basketweave No. 1

Yarn Requirements:

Orange—2 yards
Red—1 yard
Dark Rose—5 yards
Purple—4 yards
Light Green—12 yards
Dark Green—10 yards
Yellow—2 yards
Eggshell—50 yards

Five Mushrooms Pillow

(6¾" by 8½". Fig. 71 and Plate 60)

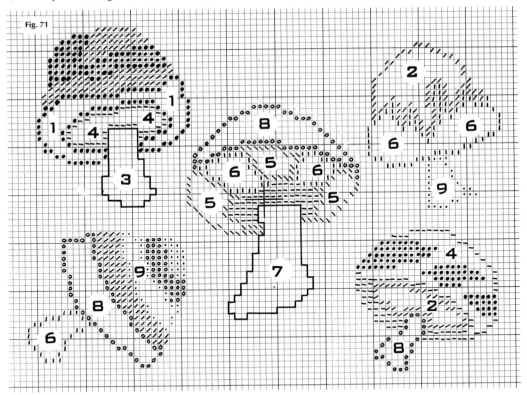

Fig. 71

Colors and Stitches:

- ● Shocking Pink Continental No. 1
- ╱ Yellow Continental No. 1
- ─ Green Continental No. 1
- ╲ Red Continental No. 1
- | Light Pink Continental No. 1
- ○ Light Blue Continental No. 1
- • Orange Continental No. 1
- 1 Shocking Pink Basketweave No. 1
- 2 Yellow Basketweave No. 1
- 3 Purple Basketweave No. 1
- 4 Green Basketweave No. 1
- 5 Red Basketweave No. 1
- 6 Light Pink Basketweave No. 1
- 7 Dark Blue Basketweave No. 1
- 8 Light Blue Basketweave No. 1
- 9 Orange Basketweave No. 1
  Background Light Tan
     Basketweave No. 1

Yarn Requirements:

Shocking Pink—2 yards
Yellow—3 yards
Green—4 yards
Red—2 yards
Light Pink—5 yards
Light Blue—4 yards
Orange—1½ yards
Purple—1½ yards
Dark Blue—2 yards
Light Tan—40 yards

Plate 60. The Three Mushrooms Tote Bag (right) represents a whimsical group of mushrooms appliquéd to a canvas tote bag. The Five Mushrooms Pillow (left) is a splash of mushrooms appliquéd to a velvet pillow. In both cases moss fringe is used to cover the raw canvas edges.

NURSERY AND WHIMSICAL DESIGNS

Humpty Dumpty Wall Hanging
(10″ by 7″. Fig. 72 and Plate 61)   Designed and Executed by William Baker

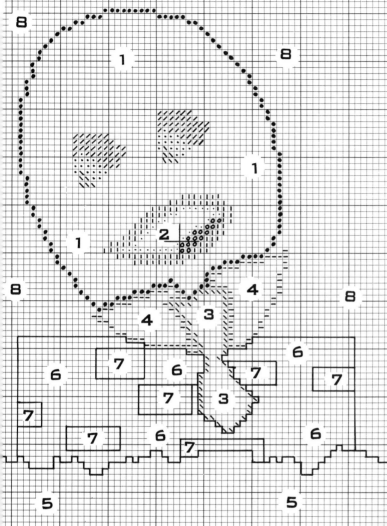

Yarn Requirements:

White—24 yards
Light Blue—2 yards
Black—7 yards
Dark Blue—3½ yards
Red—40 yards
Pink—½ yard
Light Olive—3 yards
Dark Olive—10 yards
Rust—7 yards

Plate 61. Humpty Dumpty Wall Hanging, together with the next three nursery rhymes, would make a welcome addition to any child's room. The background and grass section has been worked with the Cashmere No. 1.

Colors and Stitches:

- ● White Continental No. 1
- ╱ Light Blue Continental No. 1
- • Black Continental No. 1
- ╲ Dark Blue Continental No. 1
- | Red Continental No. 1
- ○ Pink Continental No. 1
- − Light Olive Continental No. 1
- 1 White Basketweave No. 1
- 2 Black Basketweave No. 1
- 3 Dark Blue Basketweave No. 1
- 4 Light Olive Basketweave No. 1
- 5 Dark Olive Cashmere No. 1
- 6 Rust Diagonal Mosaic No. 1
- 7 Black Mosaic No. 1
- 8 Red Cashmere No. 1

Jack and Jill Wall Hanging
(10″ by 7″. Fig. 73 and Plate 62) Designed and Executed by William Baker

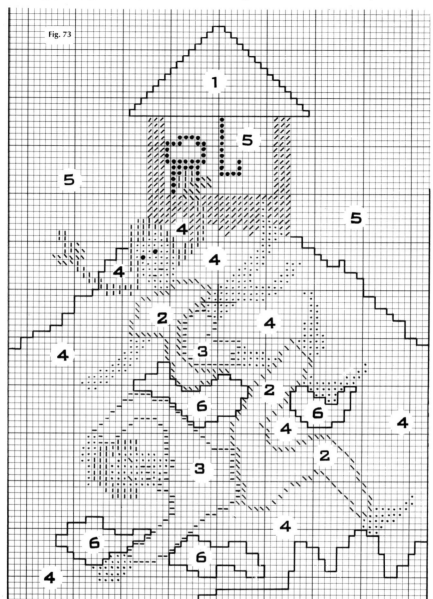

Fig. 73

Colors and Stitches:

/ Rust Continental No. 1
I Yellow Continental No. 1
\ Medium Blue Continental No. 1
— Red Continental No. 1
• Pink Continental No. 1
● Black Continental No. 1
1 Light Brown Basketweave No. 1
2 Medium Blue Basketweave No. 1
3 Red Basketweave No. 1
4 Dark Olive Diagonal Mosaic No. 1
5 Light Olive Diagonal Mosaic No. 1
6 Black Diagonal Mosaic No. 1

Yarn Requirements:

Rust—3 yards
Yellow—2 yards
Medium Blue—8 yards
Red—7 yards
Pink—8 yards
Black—10 yards
Light Brown—3 yards
Dark Olive—36 yards
Light Olive—36 yards

Plate 62. Jack and Jill Wall Hanging achieves an added sense of motion from the use of the Diagonal Mosaic No. 1 for the hill and background sky.

Little Miss Muffet Wall Hanging

(10″ by 7″. Fig. 74 and Plate 63)   Designed and Executed by William Baker

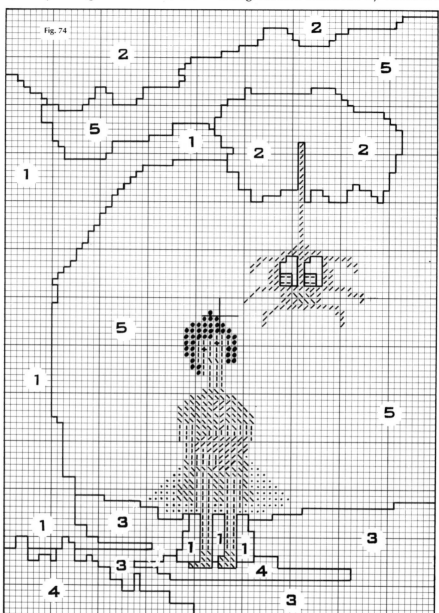

Fig. 74

Colors and Stitches:

／ Black Continental No. 1
＼ Red Continental No. 1
| Pink Continental No. 1
+ Black French Knots
● Orange Continental No. 1
• Yellow Continental No. 1
− Dark Olive Continental No. 1
1 Rust Cashmere No. 1
2 Light Olive Straight Cross
3 Dark Olive Mosaic No. 1
4 Black Continental No. 1
5 Blue Continental No. 1
Spider's Eyes Blue Continental No. 1

Yarn Requirements:

Black—6 yards
Red—2 yards
Pink—2 yards
Orange—¾ yard
Yellow—2 yards
Dark Olive—8 yards
Rust—8 yards
Light Olive—15 yards
Blue—39 yards

Plate 63. Little Miss Muffet Wall Hanging employs, in addition to the basic stitches, the Mosaic No. 1, Cashmere No. 1, and the Straight Cross. Note the particular texture of the tree leaves which results from the use of the Straight Cross.

Hickory, Dickory, Dock Wall Hanging
(10″ by 7″. Fig. 75 and Plate 64)   Designed and Executed by William Baker

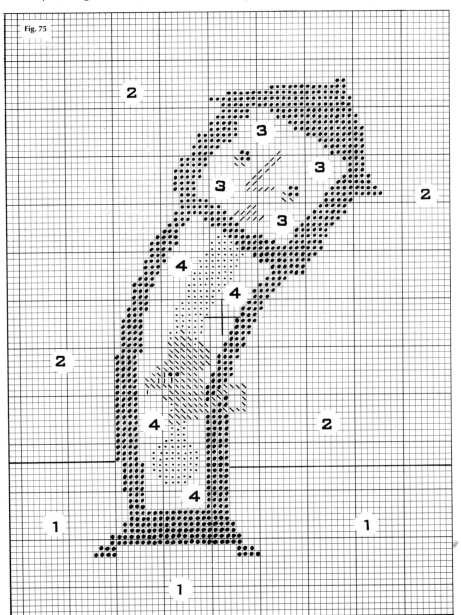

Fig. 75

Colors and Stitches:

- ● Blue Continental No. 1
- ╱ Red Continental No. 1
- ╲ Black Continental No. 1
- • Orange Continental No. 1
- I White Continental No. 1
- 1 Rust Mosaic No. 1
- 2 Yellow Mosaic No. 1
- 3 White Continental No. 1
- 4 Olive Continental No. 1

Yarn Requirements:

Blue—10 yards
Red—1 yard
Black—2 yards
Orange—3½ yards
White—3 yards
Rust—16 yards
Yellow—46 yards
Olive—5 yards

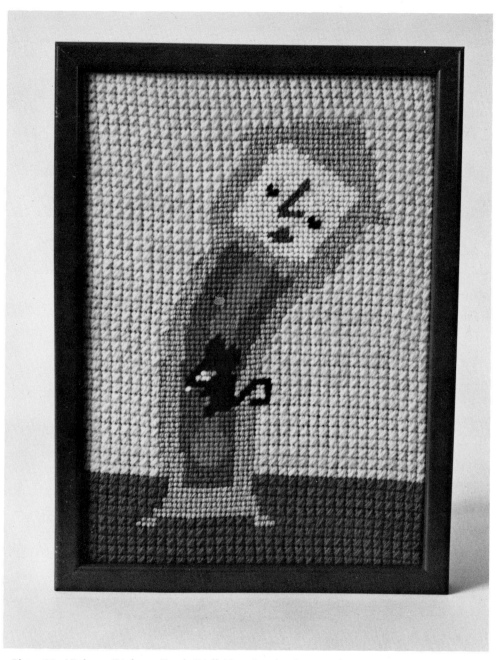

Plate 64. Hickory Dickory Dock Wall Hanging background is a rigid graph of Mosaic No. 1. This further accents the lean of the clock as he tries to look at the mouse.

Smiling Face Belt

(1⅞" wide. Fig. 76 and Plate 65)

Fig. 76

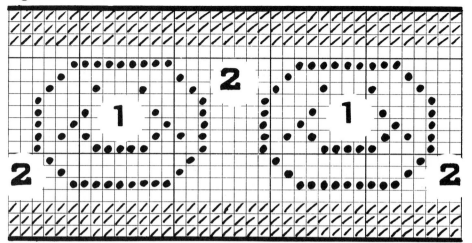

Colors and Stitches:

/ Blue Continental No. 1
● Purple Continental No. 1
1 Pink Continental No. 1
2 Eggshell Continental No. 1
Background Eggshell
  Continental No. 1

Yarn Requirements per Face:

Blue—1½ yards
Purple—1 yard
Pink—1½ yards
Eggshell—2 yards

Plate 65. The Smiling Face Belt is a study of design economy. Only 15 stitches are used to depict the mouth and eyes.

Sailboat Belt

(2⅛″ wide. Fig. 77 and Plate 66)

Fig. 77

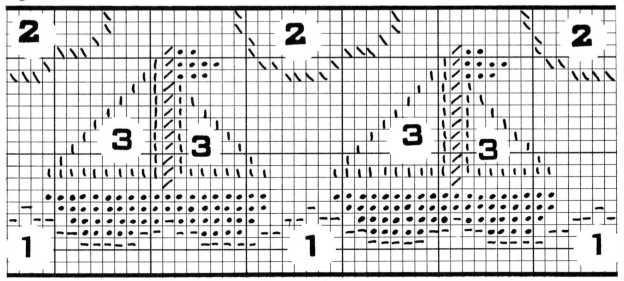

Colors and Stitches:

- Dark Blue Diagonal Mosaic No. 1
- \ Gray Continental No. 1
- • Red Continental No. 1
- / Black Continental No. 1
- I White Continental No. 1
- 1 Dark Blue Diagonal Mosaic No. 1
- 2 Gray Continental No. 1
- 3 White Continental No. 1
  Background Light Blue
    Continental No. 1

Yarn Requirements per Boat:

Dark Blue—2 yards
Gray—1 yard
Red—1 yard
Black—⅓ yard
White—1½ yards
Light Blue—3 yards

Plate 66. The Sailboat Belt is an attractive repeat design that would be suitable as an appliqué on a pillow for your own or a friend's boat. It is worked in basic red, white, and blue.

Mexican Boy Wall Hanging

(14¾ by 13¼″. Fig. 78 and Plate 67)   Designed and Executed by Linda Curtis

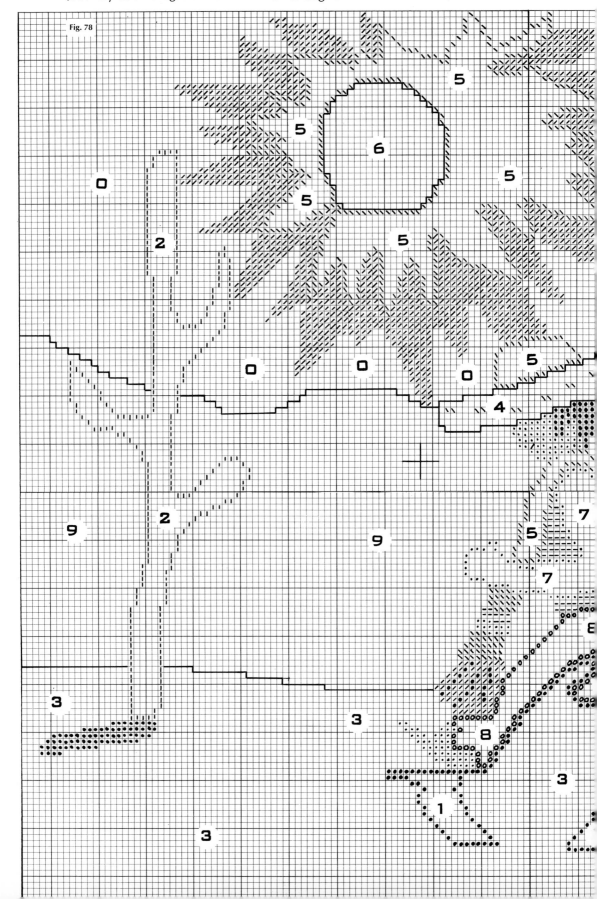

Fig. 78

Colors and Stitches:

/ Red Continental No. 1
● Black Continental No. 1
I Dark Green Continental No. 1
− Rust Continental No. 1
\ Light Orange Continental No. 1
• Flesh Continental No. 1
○ Yellow Continental No. 1
0 Light Blue Basketweave No. 1
1 Black Basketweave No. 1
2 Dark Green Basketweave No. 1
3 Light Brown Basketweave No. 1
4 Rust Basketweave No. 1
5 Light Orange Basketweave No. 1
6 Medium Orange
   Basketweave No. 1
7 Flesh Basketweave No. 1
8 Yellow Basketweave No. 1
9 Dark Brown Basketweave No. 1

Yarn Requirements:

Red—20 yards
Black—2 yards
Dark Green—6 yards
Rust—6 yards
Light Orange—14 yards
Flesh—3 yards
Yellow—5 yards
Light Brown—45 yards
Medium Orange—5 yards
Dark Brown—45 yards
Light Blue—45 yards

Plate 67. Mexican Boy Wall Hanging depicts a small Mexican boy surrounded by his native colors of red, orange, tan, brown, and a touch of green.

109

Tommy the Tiger Wall Hanging

(12″ by 12″. Fig. 79 and Plate 68)   Executed by Rena Sherman

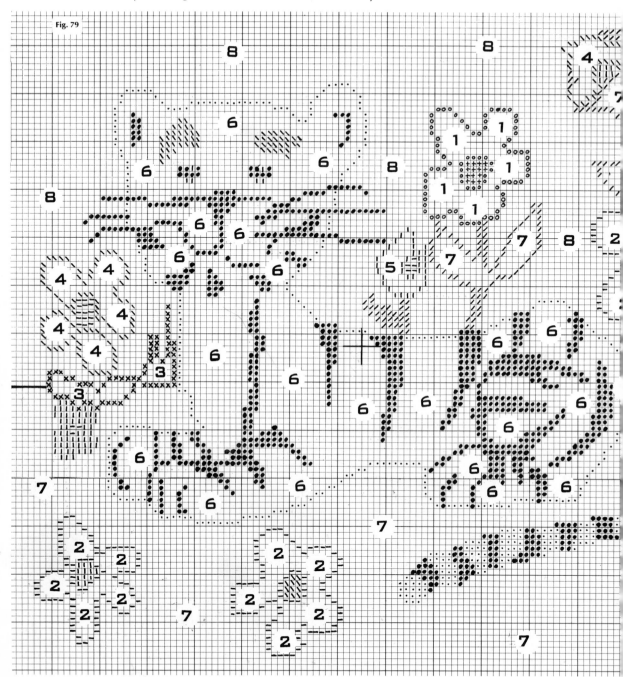

Fig. 79

Colors and Stitches:

+ Dark Raspberry Continental No. 1
○ Light Raspberry Continental No. 1
− Red Continental No. 1
× Dark Green Continental No. 1
\ Yellow Continental No. 1
| White Continental No. 1
• Orange Continental No. 1
● Black Continental No. 1
/ Light Green Continental No. 1
1 Light Raspberry Basketweave No. 1
2 Red Basketweave No. 1
3 Dark Green Basketweave No. 1
4 Yellow Basketweave No. 1
5 White Basketweave No. 1
6 Orange Basketweave No. 1
7 Light Green Basketweave No. 1
8 Blue Basketweave No. 1

Yarn Requirements:

Dark Raspberry—½ yard
Light Raspberry—2 yards
Red—8 yards
Dark Green—8 yards
Yellow—4 yards
White—3 yards
Orange—35 yards
Black—8 yards
Light Green—40 yards
Blue—40 yards

Plate 68. Tommy the Tiger Wall Hanging would hardly frighten anyone. Instead, he would make a suitable companion for that little child in your life.

Buzzing Bobby Pillow
(15″ by 15″. Fig. 80 and Plate 69)   Executed by Sue Wentz

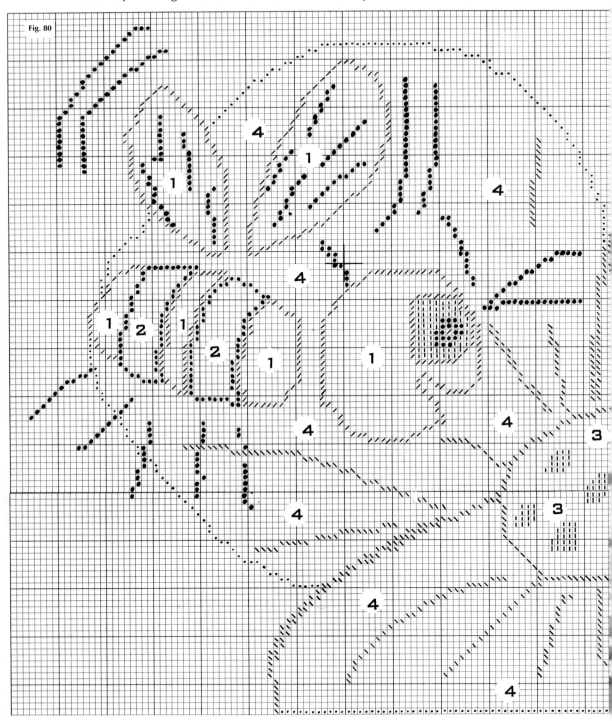

Fig. 80

Colors and Stitches:

- ● Black Continental No. 1
- ╱ Yellow Continental No. 1
- | White Continental No. 1
- ╲ Red Continental No. 1
- • Shocking Pink Continental No. 1
- 1 Yellow Basketweave No. 1
- 2 Black Basketweave No. 1
- 3 Red Basketweave No. 1
- 4 Shocking Pink
     Basketweave No. 1
     Background Light Blue
     Basketweave No. 1

Yarn Requirements:

Black—12 yards
Yellow—16 yards
White—4 yards
Red—8 yards
Shocking Pink—100 yards
Light Blue—85 yards

Plate 69. Buzzing Bobby Pillow is a companion design to Tommy the Tiger. Together they could be used as either wall hangings or pillows for a youngster or for the young at heart.

Jonah in the Whale Wall Hanging
(12″ by 12″. Fig. 81 and Plate 70)

Fig. 81

Colors and Stitches:

- − Black Continental No. 1
- / Pink Continental No. 1
- \ Light Gold Continental No. 1
- ● Gray Continental No. 1
- · White Continental No. 1
- + Brown Continental No. 1
- ○ Dark Gold Continental No. 1
- I Red Continental No. 1
- × Dark Blue French Knots
- 1 Pink Continental No. 1
- 2 Light Gold Continental No. 1
- 3 Gray Continental No. 1
- 4 Black Vertical Satin
- 5 White Continental No. 1
- 6 Dark Gold Continental No. 1
- 7 Light Blue Scotch No. 1
- 8 Medium Blue Diagonal Mosaic No. 1

Waves are Dark Blue Mosaic No. 1. The placement is only approximate since the stitches must mesh with the Medium Blue Diagonal Mosaic No. 1.

Yarn Requirements:

Black—2 yards
Pink—1 yard
Light Gold—4 yards
Gray—32 yards
White—12 yards
Brown—¾ yard
Dark Gold—3 yards
Red—¾ yard
Light Blue—35 yards
Medium Blue—28 yards
Dark Blue—38 yards

Plate 70. Jonah in the Whale, in addition to the variety of stitches, boasts the use of a variegated knitting yarn for the whale. The gray heather tone yarn reflects the light in subtle variations.

"Go Away, I'm Asleep" Wall Hanging or Pillow

(11" by 11½". Fig. 82 and Plate 71)   Executed by Rena Sherman

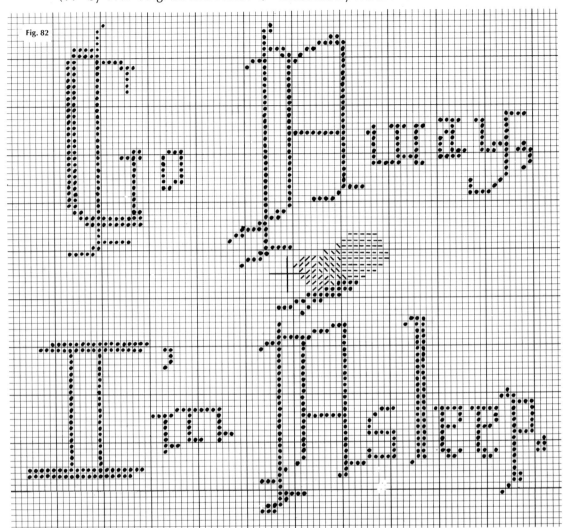

Fig. 82

Colors and Stitches:

- Black Continental No. 1
- / Light Pink Continental No. 1
- \ Red Continental No. 1
- — Dark Pink Continental No. 1
  Background Eggshell
  Basketweave No. 1

Yarn Requirements:

Black—14 yards
Light Pink—½ yard
Red—½ yard
Dark Pink—1 yard
Background—110 yards

Plate 71. The "Go Away, I'm Asleep" Wall Hanging or Pillow may be just what that sleepyhead in your life needs. It would also be clever if hung on your doorknob when you do not want to be disturbed.

Whimsical Sunburst Wall Hanging

(16'' by 16''. Fig. 83 and Plate 72)
Designed by Rose Girone, Rose's Knitting Studio, and Executed by Gertrude Eisdorfer.

Plate 72. The Whimsical Sunburst Wall Hanging is particularly suitable for the beginner. Once the outlines have been counted out, simply fill in each area with the colors indicated.

Whimsical Sunburst Wall Hanging *(continued)*

Fig. 83

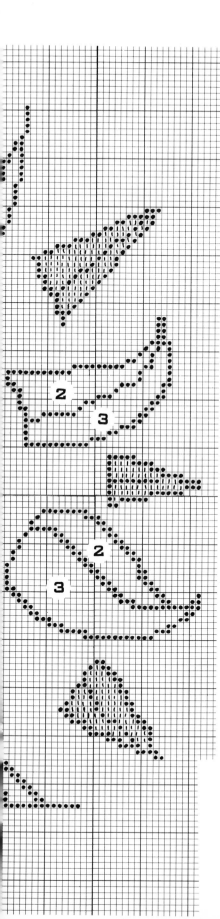

Colors and Stitches:

- Black Continental No. 1
  Outline the areas with black first, then fill each area with the colors and stitches indicated.
- Orange Continental No. 1
\ Light Red Continental No. 1
| Dark Red Continental No. 1
1 Yellow Continental No. 1
2 Orange Continental No. 1
3 Light Red Continental No. 1
  Background Light Blue
    Basketweave No. 1

Yarn Requirements:

Black—35 yards
Orange—30 yards
Light Red—30 yards
Dark Red—20 yards
Yellow—5 yards
Light Blue—150 yards

Clown Face Tote Bag

(9″ by 9″. Fig. 84 and Plate 73)

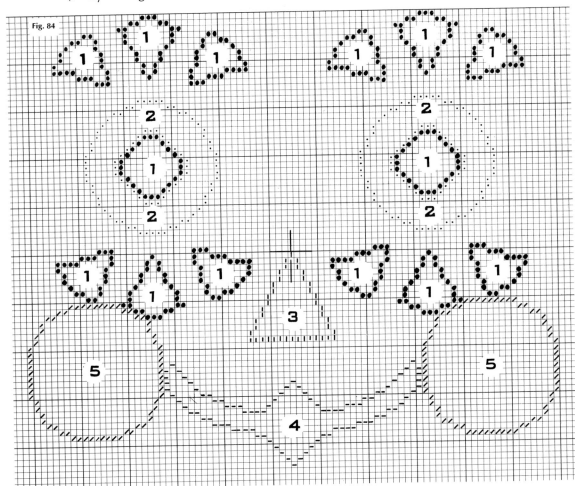

Fig. 84

Colors and Stitches:

- ● Black Continental No. 1
- • White Continental No. 1
- I Dark Blue Continental No. 1
- − Red Continental No. 1
- / Shocking Pink Continental No. 1
- 1 Black Continental No. 1
- 2 White Continental No. 1
- 3 Dark Blue Continental No. 1
- 4 Red Continental No. 1
- 5 Shocking Pink Diagonal Mosaic No. 1
  Background Medium
      Pink Scotch No. 1

Yarn Requirements:

Black—8 yards
White—6 yards
Dark Blue—2 yards
Red—4 yards
Shocking Pink—10 yards
Medium Pink—55 yards

Plate 73. The Clown Face Tote Bag would also be ideal as a youngster's pillow or as an appliqué on a notebook. The cheeks are worked with Diagonal Mosaic No. 1 and the background is worked with Scotch No. 1.

"It's Hard to Be Humble" Wall Hanging
(16″ by 10″. Fig. 85 and Plate 74)

Fig. 85

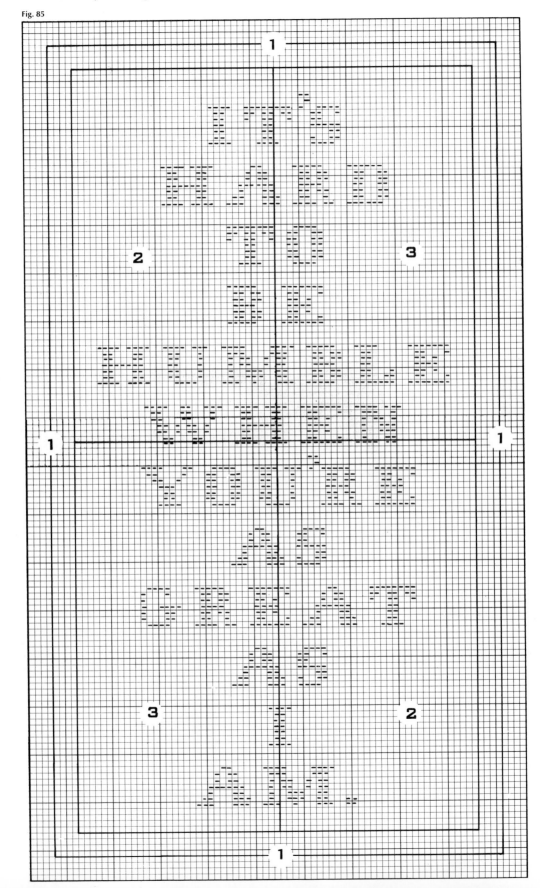

Colors and Stitches:

- Black Continental No. 1
1 Eggshell, 2 rows of Scotch No. 3 and
     Scotch No. 4
Background No. 2 is worked with
Eggshell Diagonal Mosaic No. 1.
Background No. 3 is worked with
Eggshell Diagonal Mosaic No. 2.
Outside Border is worked with Egg-
shell Stem No. 3, Stem No. 4, Slant-
ing Gobelin No. 1 and Slanting
Gobelin No. 2.

Yarn Requirements:

Black—40 yards
Eggshell—120 yards

Plate 74. "It's Hard to Be Humble" Wall Hanging will be appropriate for someone in your life as a special gift. I'm sure we all have someone we know who feels this way about himself, and needs to be reminded of his greatness.

Cinderella Sue Wall Hanging

(12″ by 11″. Fig. 86 and Plate 75)
Designed by Betsy Wansley and Executed by Joy Wansley.

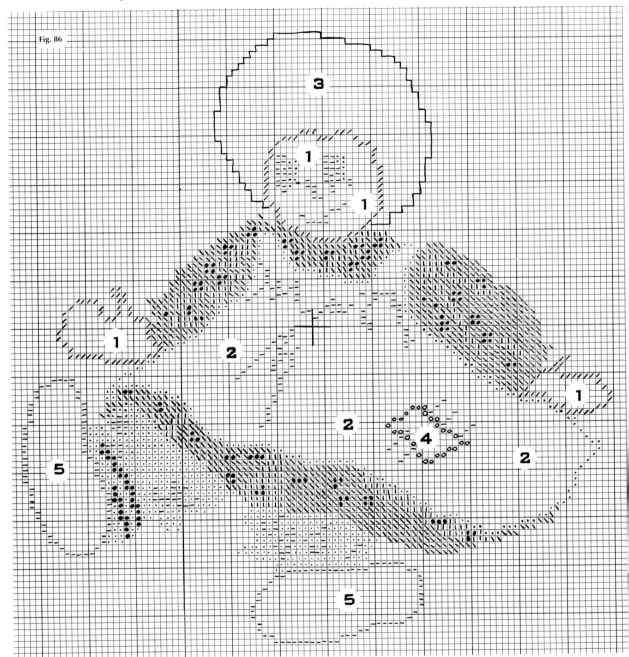

Fig. 86

Colors and Stitches:

/ Brown Continental No. 1
• White Continental No. 1
\ Dark Green Continental No. 1
| Light Green Continental No. 1
● Red Continental No. 1
– Black Continental No. 1
○ Turquoise Continental No. 1
1 Brown Basketweave No. 1
2 White Basketweave No. 1
3 Black French Knots
4 Turquoise Basketweave No. 1
5 Black Basketweave No. 1
Background Gold Cashmere No. 1

Yarn Requirements:

Brown—4 yards
White—25 yards
Black—24 yards
Light Green—3 yards
Dark Green—10 yards
Red—3 yards
Turquoise—1 yard
Gold—70 yards

Plate 75. *Cinderella Sue Wall Hanging has the greatest "natural" in the world. It is made with textured French Knots for that lifelike dimension.*

Paisley Sampler

(10¾" by 7¾". Fig. 87 and Plate 76)

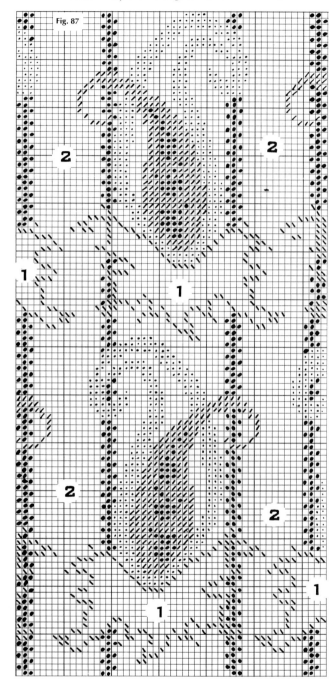

Fig. 87

Colors and Stitches:

- Gold Continental No. 1
- / Dark Rose Continental No. 1
- ● Light Rose Continental No. 1
- \ Dark Green Continental No. 1
- 1 Dark Green Basketweave No. 1
- 2 Light Green Stem No. 3
  Background Eggshell
  Continental No. 1

Yarn Requirements:

Gold—12 yards
Dark Rose—12 yards
Light Rose—10 yards
Dark Green—6 yards
Light Green—15 yards
Eggshell—15 yards

Plate 76. The Paisley Sampler would be appropriate in a variety of uses—as a pillow, bolster, piano bench cover, footstool cover, chair seat, or tote bag.

Hexagon Sampler Pillow
(15" by 15". Fig. 88 and Plate 77)

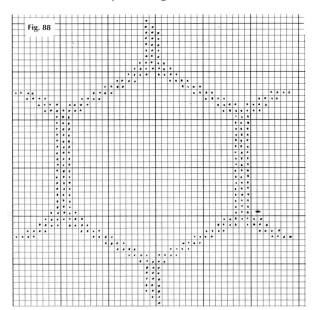

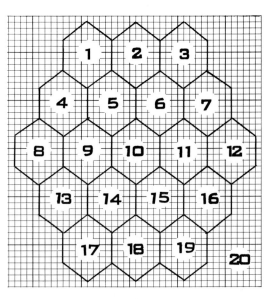

Colors and Stitches:

- Black Continental No. 1
  Work 19 hexagon motifs with Black Continental No. 1. Fill each motif with the following colors and stitches:

1 Web Stitch—3 rows of Yellow, 3 rows of Light Gold, and 3 rows of Dark Gold
2 Paris—Diagonal rows of Light Blue, Pink, and Light Purple
3 Tied—Vertical rows of Red and Rust
4 Smyrna—Alternating blocks of 4 Brown and 4 Rust
5 Straight Cross—Alternating diamonds of Dark Purple, Dark Blue, and Dark Rose
6 Milanese—Alternating rows of Yellow, Light Gold, and Brown
7 Large and Upright Cross—Dark Blue and Dark Rose
8 Double Cross—Pink and Dark Purple
9 Slanting Gobelin No. 3—Alternating rows of Pink, Shocking Pink, and Light Blue
10 Scotch No. 1—Pink and Light Purple Alternating
11 Knitting—Alternating rows of Shocking Pink and Dark Blue
12 Leaf—Alternating horizontal rows of Light Blue, Red, and Light Purple
13 Fern—Alternating rows of Yellow, Dark Gold, and Rust

14 Diagonal Mosaic No. 1—Alternating rows of Dark Blue, Dark Rose, and Dark Gold
15 Byzantine—Alternating rows of Olive, Light Blue, and Dark Purple
16 Knotted—3 rows of Dark Gold, Dark Rose, and Rust
17 Cashmere No. 1—Alternating Light Blue and Shocking Pink
18 Interlocking Gobelin—3 rows of Rust, 3 rows of Red, and 3 rows of Brown
19 Basketweave No. 1—4 rows of Yellow, 4 rows of Dark Blue, 4 rows of Pink, and in the center of this hexagon, 3 rows of Yellow
20 Basketweave No. 1—Eggshell

Yarn Requirements:

Black—50 yards
Yellow—16 yards
Light Gold—10 yards
Dark Gold—12 yards
Pink—18 yards
Light Blue—12 yards
Light Purple—20 yards
Brown—12 yards
Rust—14 yards
Red—10 yards
Dark Blue—10 yards
Dark Purple—15 yards
Dark Rose—8 yards
Shocking Pink—12 yards
Olive—8 yards
Eggshell—80 yards

Plate 77. The Hexagon Sampler Pillow is an ideal project for someone who wants to learn a variety of stitches. Each hexagon has been worked with different stitches in different colors. The pattern can be expanded or contracted as the need requires.

Stained Glass Pillow
(14″ by 14″. Fig. 89 and Plate 78)

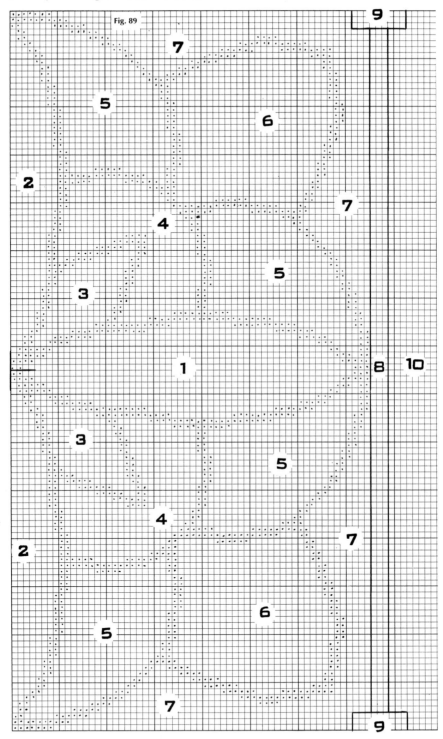

Fig. 89

Colors and Stitches:

Work the design as charted and then turn the chart upside down to work the other side.

- Gold Continental No. 1
1 Dark Blue Slanting Gobelin No. 4
2 Dark Blue Stem No. 1
3 Lavender Diagonal Mosaic No. 1
4 Light Blue Mosaic No. 1
5 Dark Rose Scotch No. 1
6 Light Rose Diagonal Mosaic No. 3
7 Light Pink Basketweave No. 1
8 Work 1 row of Navy Blue Stem No. 3 and Slanting Gobelin No. 1 around the outside edge.
9 Work 9 Navy Scotch No. 1 at each corner.
10 White Basketweave No. 1 on all sides

Yarn Requirements:

Gold—30 yards
Dark Blue—28 yards
Lavender—8 yards
Light Blue—16 yards
Dark Rose—22 yards
Light Rose—24 yards
Light Pink—32 yards
Navy—24 yards
White—50 yards

Plate 78. The Stained Glass Pillow was inspired by a 12th-century stained glass design. Each segment has been worked with different stitches.

Persian Fragment No. 1 Pillow

(10″ by 10″. Fig. 90 and Plate 79)

Fig. 90

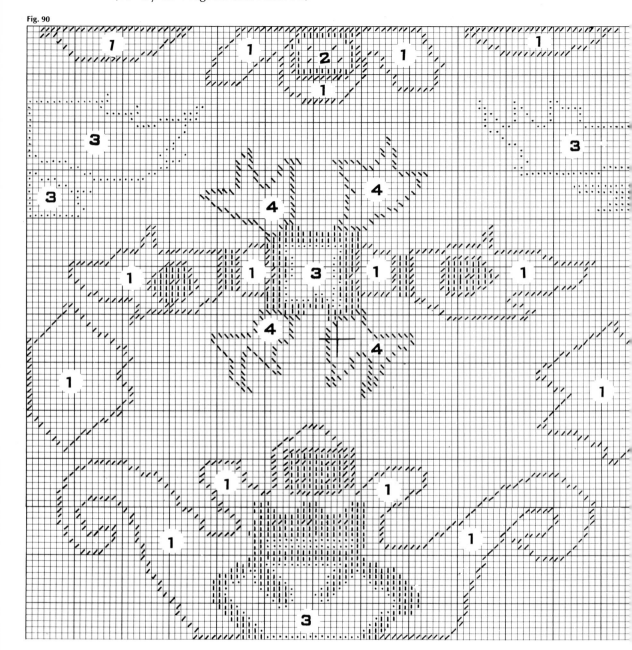

Colors and Stitches:

/ Red Continental No. 1
I Yellow Continental No. 1
• Black Continental No. 1
\ Gold Continental No. 1
1 Red Basketweave No. 1
2 Yellow Basketweave No. 1
3 Black Basketweave No. 1
4 Gold Basketweave No. 1
   Background Light Blue
   Basketweave No. 1

Yarn Requirements:

Red—25 yards
Yellow—7 yards
Black—10 yards
Gold—5 yards
Light Blue—55 yards

Persian Fragment No. 2 Pillow

(9½″ by 9″. Fig. 91 and Plate 79)

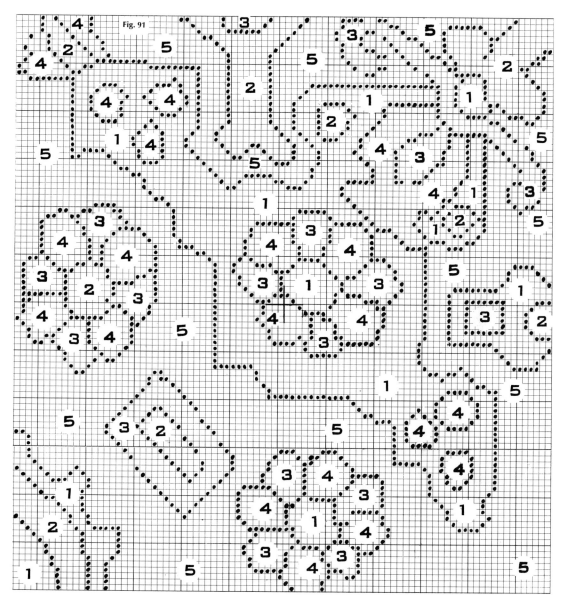

Fig. 91

Colors and Stitches:

- Red Continental No. 1
  Outline the areas with Red Continental No. 1 and then fill each area with the colors and stitches indicated.
1 Red Basketweave No. 1
2 Dark Blue Basketweave No. 1
3 Light Blue Basketweave No. 1
4 Gold Basketweave No. 1
5 Black Basketweave No. 1

Yarn Requirements:

Red—35 yards
Dark Blue—10 yards
Light Blue—10 yards
Gold—10 yards
Black—35 yards

133

Persian Fragment No. 3 Pillow

(8½" by 9". Fig. 92 and Plate 79)

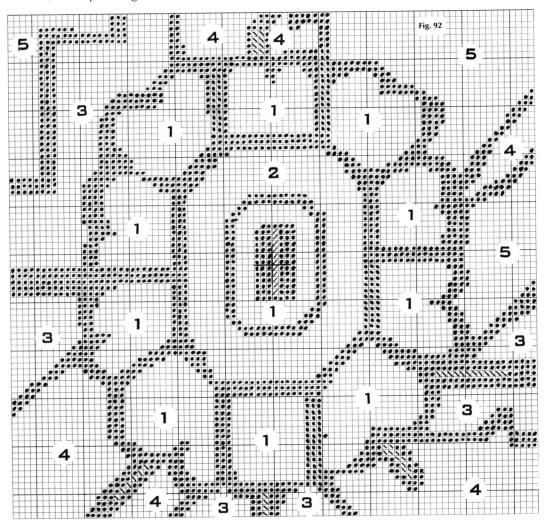

Fig. 92

Colors and Stitches:

● Black Continental No. 1
  Outline the areas with Black Continental No. 1 and then fill each area with the colors and stitches indicated.
/ Blue Continental No. 1
\ Yellow Continental No. 1
1 Blue Basketweave No. 1
2 Red Basketweave No. 1
3 Green Basketweave No. 1
4 Pink Basketweave No. 1
5 Yellow Basketweave No. 1

Yarn Requirements:

Black—35 yards
Blue—25 yards
Yellow—6 yards
Red—8 yards
Green—6 yards
Pink—9 yards

Plate 79. These three pillows were adapted from fragments of antique Persian carpets. The designs are Persian Fragment No. 1 (top), Persian Fragment No. 2 (left) and Persian Fragment No. 3 (right).

Lyre and Cross Box Top
(11″ by 15″. Fig. 93 and Plate 80)

Fig. 93

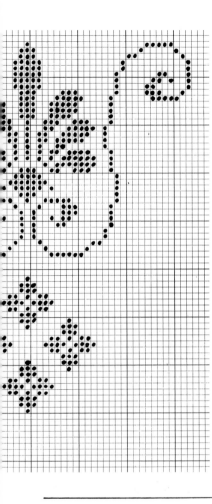

Colors and Stitches:

- Blue Continental No. 1
  Background Gold Basketweave No. 1

Yarn Requirements:

Blue—38 yards
Gold—150 yards

Griffin Box Top
(5½" by 3¼". Fig. 94 and Plate 80)

Fig. 94

Colors and Stitches:

- Black or White Continental No. 1
- / Alternate color Continental No. 1
  Background stripes in various shades
  of Gold Continental No. 1

Yarn Requirements:

Black—1½ yards per griffin
White—1½ yards per griffin
Background—12 yards

Scroll Leaf Design

(4½″ by 2¼″. Fig. 95 and Plate 80)
Designed by Alice Godkin, Woolcraft, Ltd.

Fig. 95

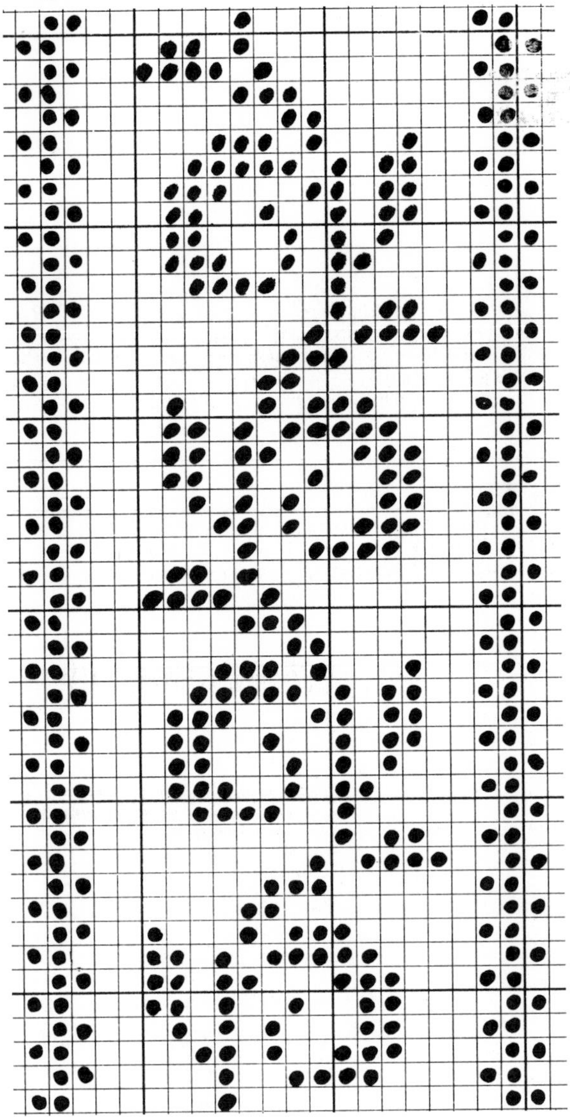

Colors and Stitches:

- Red Continental No. 1
  Background Blue Basketweave No. 1

Yarn Requirements:

Red—4 yards
Blue—8 yards

Plate 80. These classic designs would be especially appropriate for the man in your life. The designs are Lyre and Cross Box Top (left rear), Griffin Box Top (right) and Scroll Leaf Design (left front).

Fleur-de-Lys Pillow
(12″ by 12″. Fig. 96 and Plate 81)

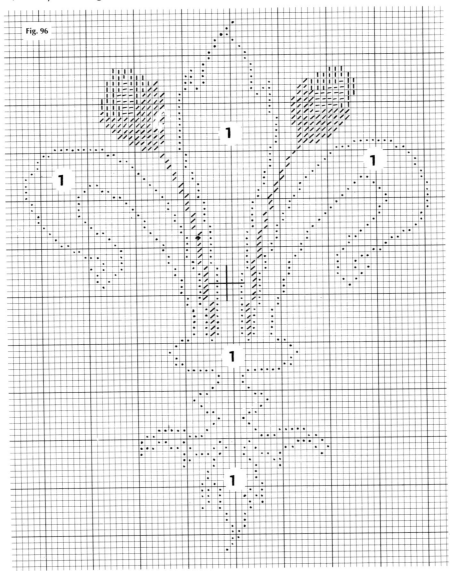

Fig. 96

Colors and Stitches:

- • White Continental No. 1
- ╱ Gold Continental No. 1
- I Dark Red Continental No. 1
- — Light Red Continental No. 1
- 1 White Basketweave No. 1
  Background Blue Basketweave No. 1

Yarn Requirements:

White—45 yards
Gold—6 yards
Light Red—¾ yard
Dark Red—1 yard
Blue—105 yards

Plate 81. The *Fleur-de-Lys Pillow* design is an adaptation of an ancient Florentine tile. This, together with the next design, would make a handsome pair of pillows.

Flambeaux Pillow

(12″ by 12″. Fig. 97 and Plate 82)

Fig. 97

Colors and Stitches:

/ Dark Gold Continental No. 1
\ Light Gold Continental No. 1
● Black Continental No. 1
• Dark Blue Continental No. 1
○ Light Blue Continental No. 1
I Dark Red Continental No. 1
— Light Red Continental No. 1
1 Dark Gold Basketweave No. 1
2 Light Gold Basketweave No. 1
3 Dark Blue Basketweave No. 1
4 Light Blue Basketweave No. 1
5 Dark Red Basketweave No. 1
6 Light Red Basketweave No. 1
Background White Basketweave No. 1

Yarn Requirements:

Dark Gold—25 yards
Light Gold—25 yards
Black—10 yards
Dark Blue—15 yards
Light Blue—6 yards
Dark Red—6 yards
Light Red—6 yards
White—65 yards

Plate 82. The Flambeaux Pillow is vibrant with its shades of blue, gold, and red. This classic design is another that is particularly suited for the man's room.

143

Fleur-de-Lys and Cross Box Top, Chairback, Pincushion, or Sachet

(Box Top 4 1/8″ by 3 4/5″. Fig. 98 and Plate 83)

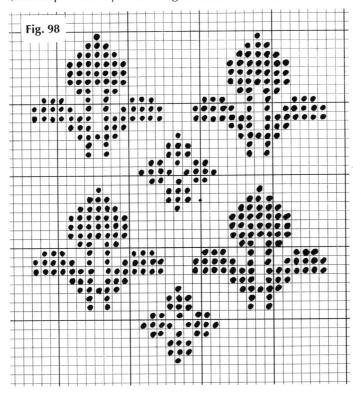

Fig. 98

Colors and Stitches:

- ● Gold Continental No. 1
  Background Brown
     Basketweave No. 1

Yarn Requirements for Box Top:

Gold—½ yard per cross and 1 yard per
     fleur-de-lys
Brown—1 yard per square inch

Plate 83. The Fleur-de-Lys and Cross design has been used for a chair back, box top and pincushion. Many small repeat designs have this marvelous adaptability for use on either very small projects or extended to cover very large projects.

145

Paisley Eyeglass Case or Checkbook Cover

(6¾" by 3½". Fig. 99 and Plate 84)

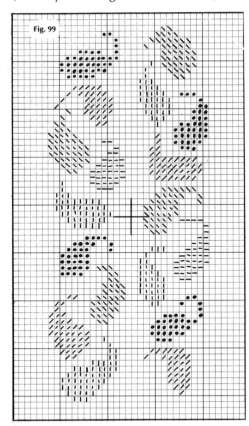

Colors and Stitches:

- ● Pink Continental No. 1
- / Yellow Continental No. 1
- \ Green Continental No. 1
- I Red Continental No. 1
- — Blue Continental No. 1
  Background Black Basketweave No. 1

Yarn Requirements per Side:

Pink—1 yard
Yellow—1 yard
Green—1 yard
Red—1 yard
Blue—1 yard
Black—20 yards

Plate 84. The Paisley Eyeglass Case or Checkbook Cover design is worked with bright colors on a black background. Each Paisley glows like a jewel in a dark setting. The design could be extended to cover many larger projects with equal effectiveness.

Comet 1906 Wall Hanging

(8'' by 10''. Fig. 100 and Plate 85)   Designed and Executed by William Baker

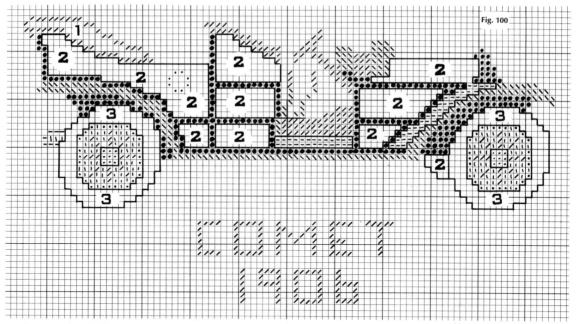

Colors and Stitches:

/   Light Brown Continental No. 1
●   Dark Olive Continental No. 1
—   Light Olive Continental No. 1
•   Black Continental No. 1
\   Yellow Continental No. 1
| Eggshell Continental No. 1
1   Light Brown Basketweave No. 1
2   Light Olive Basketweave No. 1
3   Blue Basketweave No. 1
    Background Eggshell Mosaic No. 1

Yarn Requirements:

Light Brown—3½ yards
Dark Olive—4 yards
Light Olive—8 yards
Black—2½ yards
Yellow—½ yard
Blue—3½ yards
Eggshell—80 yards

Plate 85. The Comet 1906 Wall Hanging, together with the next design, would be stunning in the den. Each is particularly suited to the masculine atmosphere.

Keeton 1913 Wall Hanging

(8″ by 10″. Fig. 101 and Plate 86)   Designed and Executed by William Baker

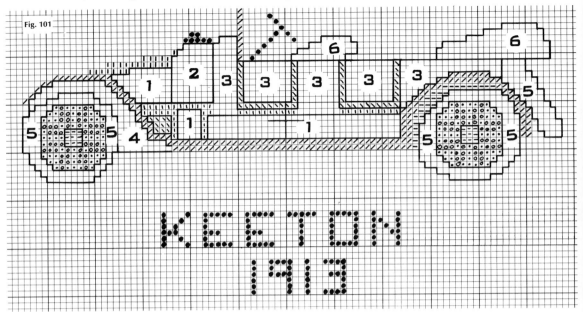

Fig. 101

Colors and Stitches:

/ Dark Purple Continental No. 1
\ Light Purple Continental No. 1
| Medium Blue Continental No. 1
− Raspberry Continental No. 1
• Brown Continental No. 1
● Orange Continental No. 1
○ Eggshell Continental No. 1
1 Light Purple Basketweave No. 1
2 Light Blue Basketweave No. 1
3 Medium Blue Basketweave No. 1
4 Raspberry Basketweave No. 1
5 Black Basketweave No. 1
6 Brown Basketweave No. 1
  Background Eggshell Mosaic No. 1

Yarn Requirements:

Dark Purple—1½ yards
Light Purple—3½ yards
Medium Blue—1 yard
Raspberry—2 yards
Brown—3 yards
Orange—2 yards
Light Blue—1 yard
Black—3½ yards
Eggshell—90 yards

Plate 86. The Keeton 1913 Wall Hanging, together with the previous design, gain considerable interest from the use of the Mosaic No. 1 and No. 2 stitches as background. This larger stitch lends a certain ruggedness to each of the designs.

Napoleonic Bee Box Top or Wall Hanging

(Each bee measures 1 7/10″ by 1 1/3″ and they are spaced 1″ above one another with 1 1/5″ between each other. Fig. 102 and Plate 87)

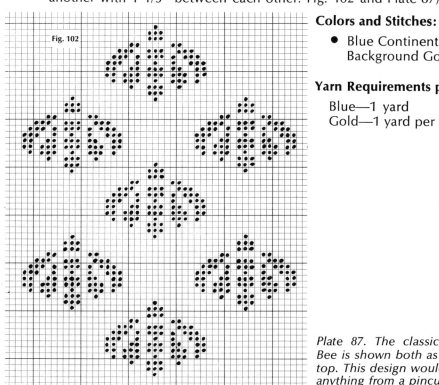

Fig. 102

Colors and Stitches:

- Blue Continental No. 1
  Background Gold Basketweave No. 1

Yarn Requirements per Bee:

Blue—1 yard
Gold—1 yard per square inch

Plate 87. The classically simple Napoleonic Bee is shown both as a wall hanging and box top. This design would be effective on almost anything from a pincushion to a rug.

Pre-Columbian Medallion Pillow
(11″ by 11″. Fig. 103 and Plate 88)

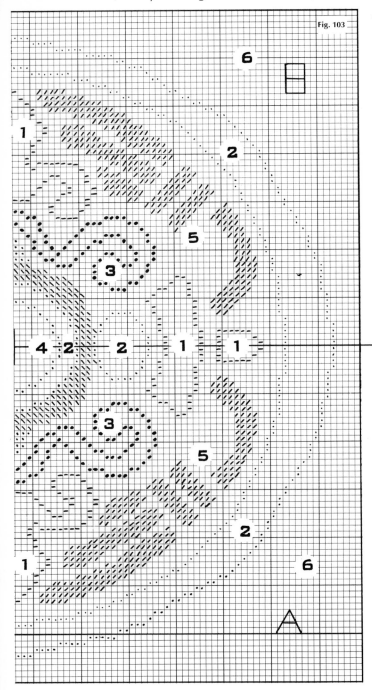

Fig. 103

Colors and Stitches:

Work the design as charted and then turn the chart upside down to work the other side. A corners are worked in No. 1 stitches and B corners are worked in No. 2 stitches.

/ Medium Brown Continental No. 1 and Continental No. 2

− Dark Red Continental No. 1 and Continental No. 2

• Gold Continental No. 1 and Continental No. 2

\ Black Continental No. 1 and Continental No. 2

● Green Continental No. 1 and Continental No. 2

1 Dark Red Basketweave No. 1 and Basketweave No. 2

2 Gold Basketweave No. 1 and Basketweave No. 2

3 Green Basketweave No. 1 and Basketweave No. 2

4 Eggshell Basketweave No. 1 and Basketweave No. 2

5 Background inside Gold Circle Eggshell Basketweave No. 1 and Basketweave No. 2

6 Dark Brown Scotch No. 3 and Scotch No. 4

Yarn Requirements:

Medium Brown—36 yards
Dark Rose—10 yards
Gold—20 yards
Green—6 yards
Black—2 yards
Eggshell—30 yards
Dark Brown—30 yards

Plate 88. The Pre-Columbian Medallion Pillow was inspired by a Pre-Columbian stone carving. The symmetry of the design is further enhanced by changing the direction of the stitches in each of the four quarters.

Flying Bee Wall Hanging

(6½″ by 6½″. Fig. 104 and Plate 89)

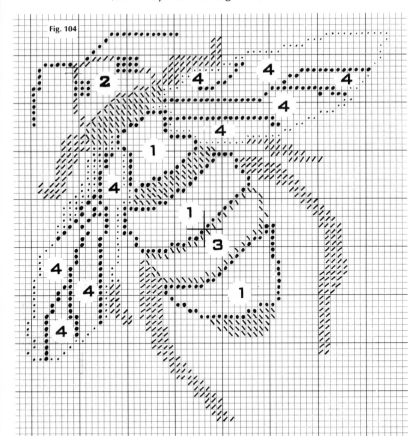

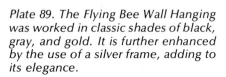

Colors and Stitches:

- ● Black Continental No. 1
- • Gray Continental No. 1
- / Dark Gold
    Continental No. 1
- \ Light Gold
    Continental No. 1
- 1 Black Basketweave No. 1
- 2 Dark Gold
    Basketweave No. 1
- 3 Light Gold
    Basketweave No. 1
- 4 Gray Basketweave No. 1
    Background Eggshell
    Basketweave No. 1

Yarn Requirements:

Black—7 yards
Gray—3 yards
Dark Gold—5 yards
Light Gold—6 yards
Eggshell—24 yards

*Plate 89. The Flying Bee Wall Hanging
was worked in classic shades of black,
gray, and gold. It is further enhanced
by the use of a silver frame, adding to
its elegance.*

Folded Ribbon Belt

(2″ wide. Fig. 105 and Plate 90)

Fig. 105

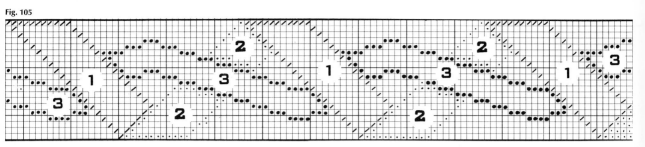

Colors and Stitches:

/ Dark Blue Continental No. 1
• Light Blue Continental No. 1
● Yellow Continental No. 1
1 Dark Blue Basketweave No. 1
2 Light Blue Basketweave No. 1
3 Yellow Basketweave No. 1
 Background Gold Basketweave No. 1

Yarn Requirements:

Dark Blue—2 yards
Light Blue—1½ yards
Yellow—2 yards
Gold—4 yards

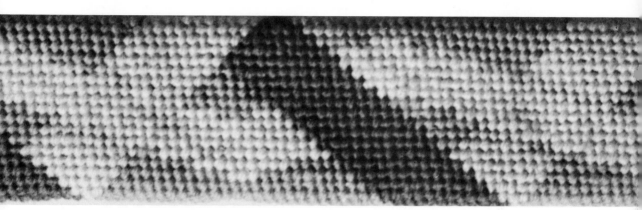

Plate 90. The folded Ribbon Belt intertwines itself in an optical illusion. What an attractive luggage rack strap this would make.

Still Life Wall Hanging

(10″ by 10″. Fig. 106 and Plate 91)   Executed by Rena Sherman

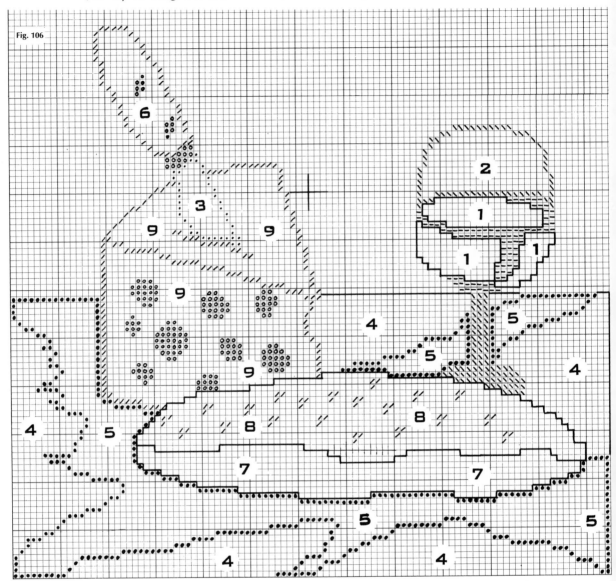

Fig. 106

Plate 91. The Still Life Wall Hanging depicts the classic combination of bread, cheese, and wine. Each has been painted in realistic detail.

Colors and Stitches:

- − Light Rose Continental No. 1
- \\ White Continental No. 1
- • Gray Continental No. 1
- ● Dark Blue Continental No. 1
- / Black Continental No. 1
- ○ Dark Yellow Continental No. 1
- 1 Dark Rose Basketweave No. 1
- 2 White Basketweave No. 1
- 3 Gray Basketweave No. 1
- 4 Light Blue Basketweave No. 1
- 5 Dark Blue Basketweave No. 1
- 6 Black Basketweave No. 1
- 7 Medium Tan Basketweave No. 1
- 8 Medium Brown Basketweave No. 1
- 9 Light Yellow Basketweave No. 1
  Background Light Tan
  Basketweave No. 1

Yarn Requirements:

Light Rose—¾ yard
White—3 yards
Gray—1 yard
Black—5 yards
Dark Yellow—3 yards
Dark Rose—2 yards
Light Blue—15 yards
Dark Blue—16 yards
Medium Tan—5 yards
Medium Brown—5 yards
Light Yellow—8 yards
Light Tan—33 yards

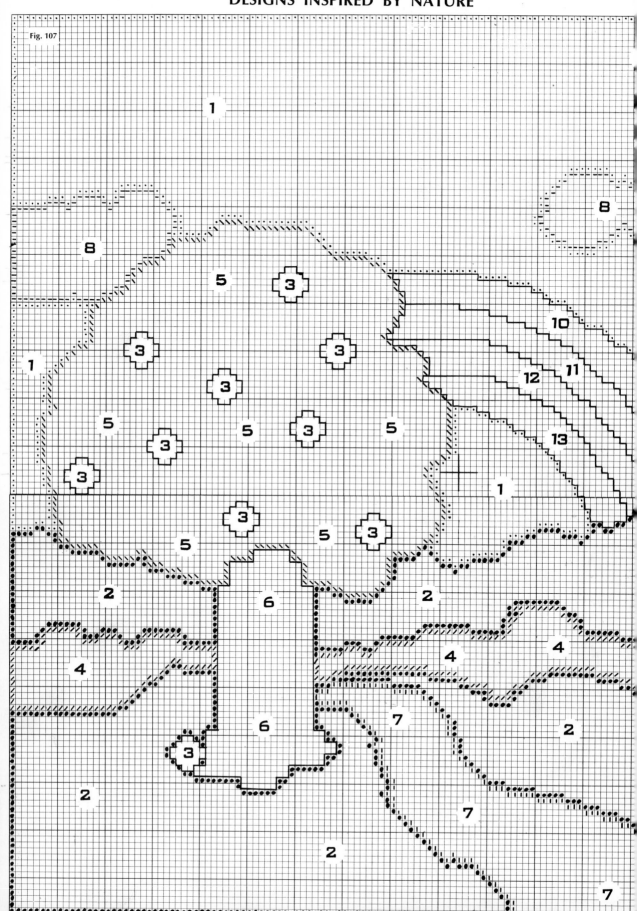

Fig. 107

Country Scene Wall Hanging (15″ by 15″. Fig. 107 and Plate 92)

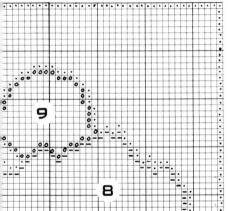

Colors and Stitches:

- • Medium Blue Continental No. 1
- ● Light Green Continental No. 1
- / Dark Green Continental No. 1
- \ Dark Green Diagonal Mosaic No. 1
- I Light Brown Straight Cross
- — Gray Straight Cross
- ○ Light Orange Diagonal Mosaic No. 1
- 1 Medium Blue Continental No. 1
- 2 Light Green Continental No. 1
- 3 Red Vertical Satin
- 4 Dark Green Continental No. 1
- 5 Dark Green Diagonal Mosaic No. 1
- 6 Dark Brown Mosaic No. 1
- 7 Light Brown Straight Cross
- 8 Gray Straight Cross
- 9 Light Orange Diagonal Mosaic No. 1
- 10 Red Diagonal Mosaic No. 1
- 11 Dark Rose Diagonal Mosaic No. 1
- 12 Medium Orange Diagonal Mosaic No. 1
- 13 Yellow Diagonal Mosaic No. 1

Yarn Requirements:

Medium Blue—65 yards
Light Green—70 yards
Dark Green—65 yards
Light Brown—10 yards
Gray—8 yards
Light Orange—1½ yards
Red—4 yards
Dark Brown—4 yards
Light Orange—2 yards
Dark Rose—2 yards
Medium Orange—2 yards
Yellow—2 yards

Plate 92. The Country Scene fairly sings with color and texture. The Satin Stitch apples are worked on a vibrant green Diagonal Mosaic Stitch. The heathery gray clouds are worked with Straight Cross Stitch and the rainbow sings in brilliant bands of Diagonal Mosaic No. 1.

Zebra Skin Eyeglass Case or Checkbook Cover

(6¾″ by 3½″. Fig. 108 and Plate 93)

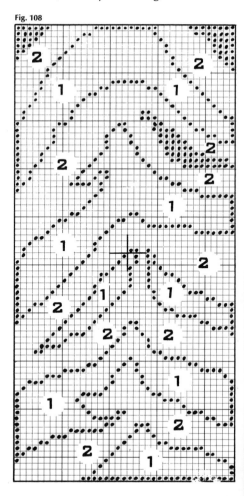

Fig. 108

Colors and Stitches:

- ● Black Continental No. 1
- 1 Black Basketweave No. 1
- 2 White Basketweave No. 1

Yarn Requirements for One Side:

Black—12 yards
White—12 yards

Plate 93. The Zebra Skin Eyeglass Case or Checkbook Cover gains its simple elegance from its restrained use of black and white. If worked in rust and black it would resemble a tiger skin.

158

Rainbow Coaster

(3½" by 3½". Fig. 109 and Plate 94)

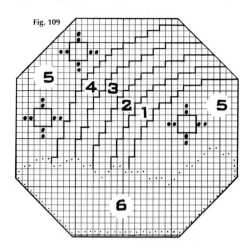

Fig. 109

Colors and Stitches:

- • Black Continental No. 1
- ● White Continental No. 1
- ▢ White Scotch No. 1
- 1 Red Horizontal Satin
- 2 Yellow Horizontal Satin
- 3 Dark Purple Satin
- 4 Pink Horizontal Satin
- 5 Blue Stem No. 2
- 6 White Diagonal Mosaic No. 1

Yarn Requirements:

White—3 yards
Blue—4 yards
Red—1 yard
Yellow—1 yard
Dark Purple—1 yard
Pink—1 yard

Dog Eyeglass Case or Checkbook Cover

(4¾" by 7¾". Fig. 110 and Plate 94)

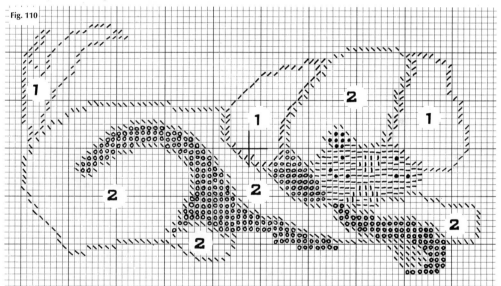

Fig. 110

Colors and Stitches:

/ Rust Continental No. 1
\ Medium Brown Continental No. 1
● Dark Brown Continental No. 1
− White Continental No. 1
I Red Continental No. 1
○ Gold Continental No. 1
1 Rust Basketweave No. 1
2 Medium Brown Basketweave No. 1
Background Light Brown
　　Basketweave No. 1

Yarn Requirements for One Side:

Rust—5 yards
Medium Brown—10 yards
Dark Brown—2 yards
White—1 yard
Red—½ yard
Gold—¾ yard
Light Brown—17 yards

Pink Elephant Eyeglass Case or Checkbook Cover

(6¾" by 4¼". Fig. 111 and Plate 94)

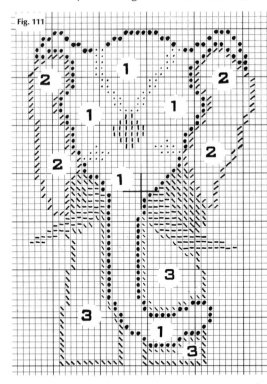

Fig. 111

Colors and Stitches:

- ● Shocking Pink Continental No. 1
- ╱ Dark Pink Continental No. 1
- • Blue Continental No. 1
- I Red Continental No. 1
- — White Continental No. 1
- ╲ Medium Pink Continental No. 1
- 1 Shocking Pink Basketweave No. 1
- 2 Dark Pink Basketweave No. 1
- 3 Medium Pink Basketweave No. 1
  Background Light Brown
    Basketweave No. 1

Yarn Requirements for One Side:

Shocking Pink—8 yards
Dark Pink—6 yards
Blue—1 yard
Red—½ yard
White—1½ yards
Medium Pink—6 yards
Light Brown—10 yards

Turtle Eyeglass Case or Checkbook Cover

(4" by 6". Fig. 112 and Plate 94)

Colors and Stitches:

- ✕ Black Continental No. 1
- ╱ Gold Continental No. 1
- I Orange Continental No. 1
- ● Yellow Continental No. 1
- — Green Continental No. 1
- 1 Gold Basketweave No. 1
- 2 Orange Basketweave No. 1
- 3 Yellow Basketweave No. 1
- 4 Purple Basketweave No. 1
- 5 Red Basketweave No. 1
- 6 Green Basketweave No. 1
  Background Light Brown
    Basketweave No. 1

Fig. 112

Yarn Requirements for One Side:

Black—⅛ yard
Gold—3 yards
Orange—1⅓ yards
Yellow—4 yards
Green—2 yards
Purple—1½ yards
Red—1½ yards
Light Brown—10 yards

Plate 94. These small projects make ideal bazaar or quick gift items. The designs are *Rainbow Coaster* (lower left), *Dog Eyeglass Case or Checkbook Cover* (lower right), *Pink Elephant Eyeglass Case or Checkbook Cover* (upper left), *and Turtle Eyeglass Case or Checkbook Cover* (upper right).

Fish and Starfish Pillow
(9" by 9". Fig. 113 and Plate 95)   Executed by Rena Sherman

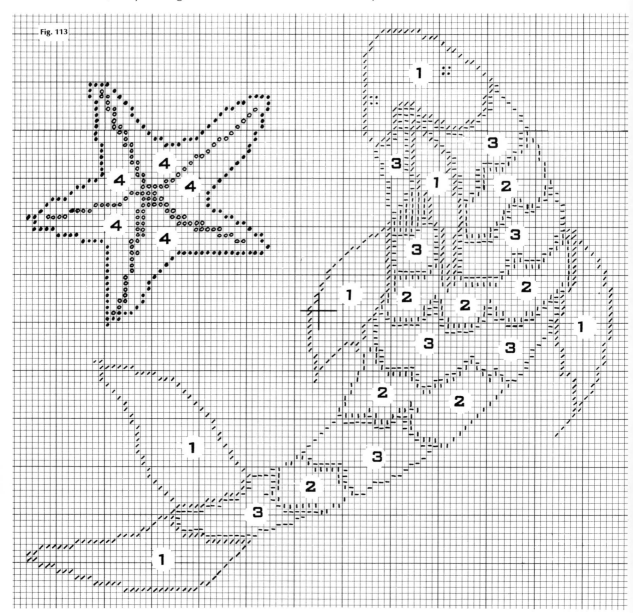

Fig. 113

Colors and Stitches:

/ Dark Blue Continental No. 1
I Light Green Continental No. 1
— Dark Green Continental No. 1
● Light Brown Continental No. 1
○ Dark Brown Continental No. 1
• Black Continental No. 1
1 Dark Blue Basketweave No. 1
2 Light Green Basketweave No. 1
3 Dark Green Basketweave No. 1
4 Light Brown Basketweave No. 1
   Background Light Blue
      Basketweave No. 1

Yarn Requirements:

Dark Blue—12 yards
Light Green—12 yards
Dark Green—12 yards
Light Brown—5 yards
Dark Brown—2 yards
Black—⅓ yard
Light Blue—45 yards

Plate 95. The Fish and Starfish Pillow has been worked in muted shades of blue and green. The repeated curves in the design lend a feeling of motion to the overall composition.

Tiger Skin Pillow

(10½″ by 10½″. Fig. 114 and Plate 96)

Fig. 114

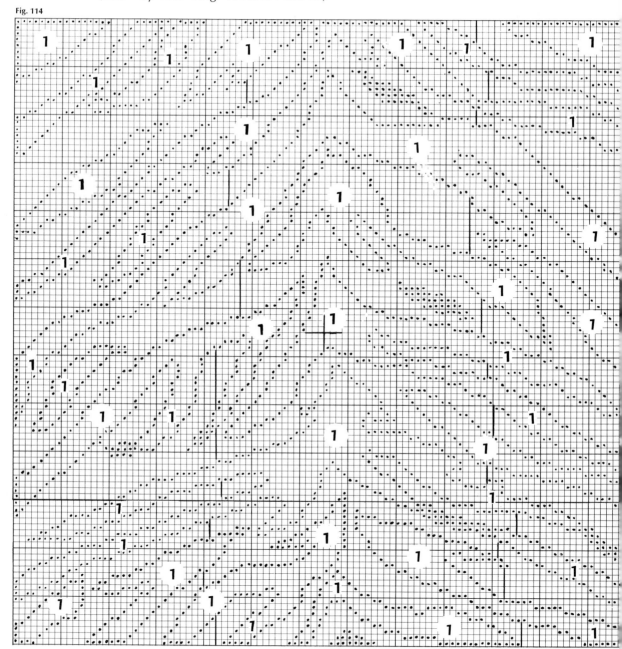

Colors and Stitches:

- Black Continental No. 1
1 Black Basketweave No. 1
  Background Center Light Rust
    Basketweave No. 1
  Background Outside Edges Light Rust
    Basketweave No. 1

Yarn Requirements:

Black—40 yards
Light Rust—40 yards
Dark Rust—40 yards

Plate 96. The Tiger Skin Pillow, together with the following design, are classic designs inspired by nature. Each, in its simplicity, is stunning.

Zebra Skin Pillow

(10½″ by 10½″. Fig. 115 and Plate 97)

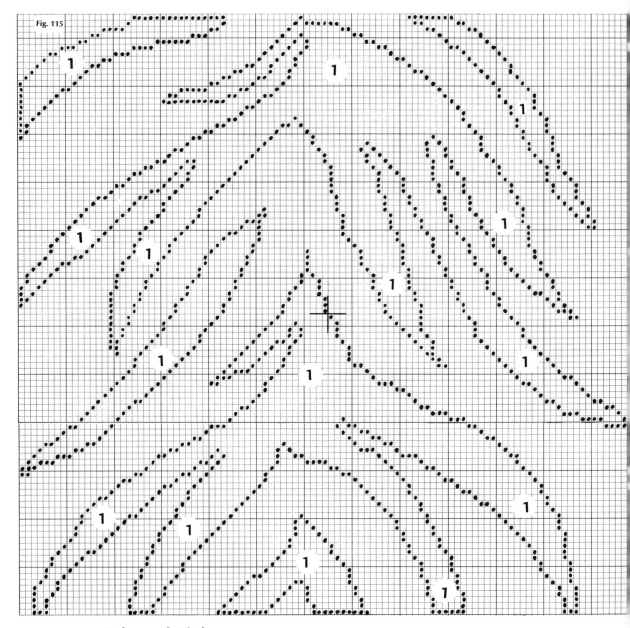

Fig. 115

Colors and Stitches:

● Black Continental No. 1
1 Black Basketweave No. 1
   Background White Basketweave No. 1

Yarn Requirements:

Black—45 yards
White—65 yards

Plate 97. The Zebra Skin Pillow, together with the preceding design, would be equally effective if worked in a variety of stitches—Diagonal Mosaic, Diagonal Cashmere, Gobelin, just to name a few.

Leopard Face Pillow
(11" by 11". Fig. 116 and Plate 98)

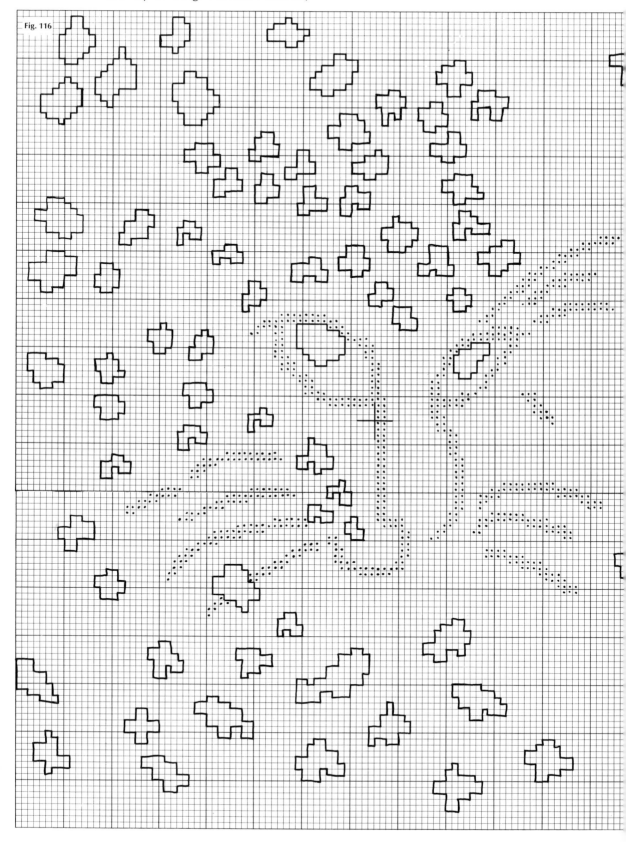

Fig. 116

Colors and Stitches:

- Black Continental No. 1
  Outlined Areas (Spots and Center of
    Eyes) Vertical Satin
  Background Eggshell
    Basketweave No. 1

Yarn Requirements:

Black—40 yards
Eggshell—80 yards

Plate 98. The Leopard Face Pillow is a study in simplicity. A few lines and a few spots suggest the jungle cat in all its cunning and beauty.

169

ZODIAC DESIGNS
Designed by William Baker

Capricorn—December 22 through January 19
(6" by 6". Fig. 117 and Plate 99)

Fig. 117

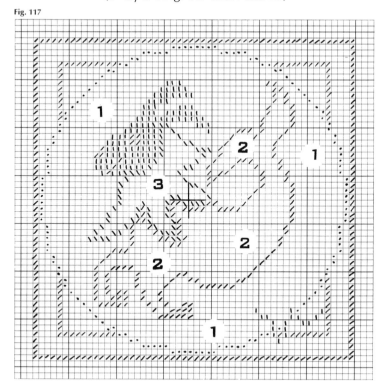

Colors and Stitches:

- • Eggshell Continental No. 1
- ∕ Dark Blue Continental No. 1
- ∖ Light Blue Continental No. 1
- I Gold Continental No. 1
- 1 Eggshell Basketweave No. 1
- 2 Dark Blue Continental No. 1
- 3 Light Blue Continental No. 1
  Outside Border Light Green Scotch No. 1 is worked between the rows of Dark Blue Continental No. 1.

Yarn Requirements:

Dark Blue—7 yards
Light Blue—3 yards
Gold—1 yard
Eggshell—20 yards
Light Green—6 yards

Aquarius—January 20 through February 18
(6" by 6". Fig. 118 and Plate 99)

Fig. 118

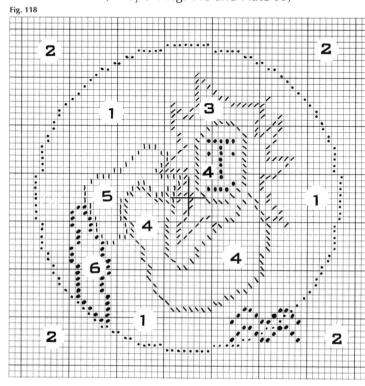

Colors and Stitches:

- • Eggshell Continental No. 1
- ∕ Gray Continental No. 1
- ∖ Pink Continental No. 1
- ● Dark Blue Continental No. 1
- I Rust Continental No. 1
- 1 Eggshell Basketweave No. 1
- 2 Alternating rows of Stem No. 1 and Stem No. 2 in Dark Rose and 2 rows of Continental No. 1 in Light Rose.
- 3 Gray Basketweave No. 1
- 4 Pink Basketweave No. 1
- 5 Rust Basketweave No. 1
- 6 Dark Blue Basketweave No. 1

Yarn Requirements:

Eggshell—20 yards
Gray—2 yards
Pink—3 yards
Dark Blue—2 yards
Rust—2 yards
Light Rose—4 yards
Dark Rose—4 yards

Pisces—February 19 through March 20
(6" by 6". Fig. 119 and Plate 99)

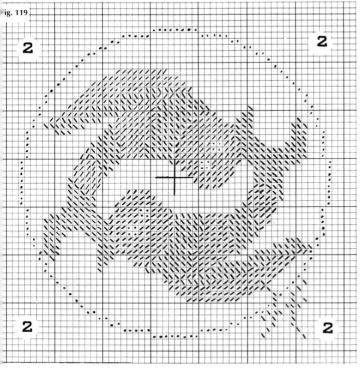

Fig. 119

Colors and Stitches:

- • Eggshell Continental No. 1
- / Light Blue Continental No. 1
- \ Dark Blue Continental No. 1
- 1 Eggshell Basketweave No. 1
- 2 Olive Scotch No. 1

Yarn Requirements:

Eggshell—20 yards
Light Blue—5 yards
Dark Blue—5 yards
Olive—6 yards

Aries—March 21 through April 19
(6" by 6". Fig. 120 and Plate 99)

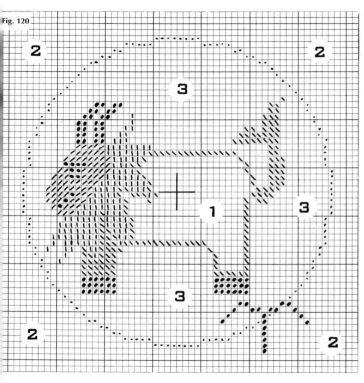

Fig. 120

Colors and Stitches:

- • Eggshell Continental No. 1
- / Dark Pink Continental No. 1
- ● Gray Continental No. 1
- I Light Pink Continental No. 1
- / Medium Rose Continental No. 1
- 1 Medium Rose
     Basketweave No. 1
- 2 Dark Rose Scotch No. 1 and
     Scotch No. 2 Alternating
- 3 Eggshell Continental No. 1

Yarn Requirements:

Eggshell—20 yards
Dark Pink—1 yard
Gray—¾ yard
Light Pink—1 yard
Medium Rose—5 yards
Dark Rose—10 yards

171

Plate 99. The Zodiac Designs are Capricorn (lower left), Aquarius (far right), Pisces (center front) and Aries (rear). They have been made into box tops, pincushions, and wall hangings.

Taurus—April 20 through May 20

(6″ by 6″. Fig. 121 and Plate 100)

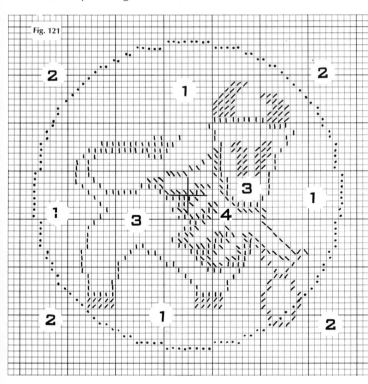

Fig. 121

Colors and Stitches:

- Eggshell Continental No. 1
/ Gold Continental No. 1
  Dark Rose Continental No. 1
  Pink Continental No. 1
1 Eggshell Basketweave No. 1
2 Two rows of Light Green Stem No. 1 and Stem No. 2 alternating with two rows of Dark Green Stem No. 1 and Stem No. 2
3 Dark Rose Basketweave No. 1
4 Pink Basketweave No. 1

Yarn Requirements:

Eggshell—20 yards
Gold—1 yard
Dark Rose—5 yards
Pink—2 yards
Light Green—4 yards
Dark Green—4 yards

Gemini—May 21 through June 20

(6″ by 6″. Fig. 122 and Plate 100)

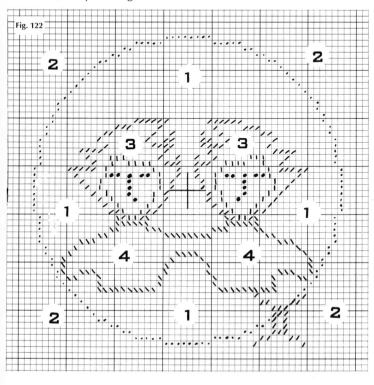

Fig. 122

Colors and Stitches:

- Eggshell Continental No. 1
/ Gold Continental No. 1
| Pink Continental No. 1
• Dark Blue Continental No. 1
\ Dark Rose Continental No. 1
1 Eggshell Basketweave No. 1
2 Light and Dark Blue Scotch No. 1 Alternating
3 Gold Basketweave No. 1
4 Dark Rose Basketweave No. 1

Yarn Requirements:

Eggshell—21 yards
Gold—2 yards
Pink—2 yards
Dark Blue—4 yards
Dark Rose—4 yards
Light Blue—4 yards

Cancer—June 21 through July 22

(6″ by 6″. Fig. 123 and Plate 100)

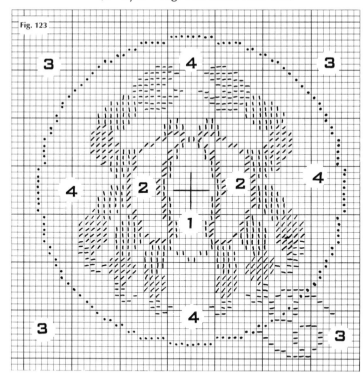

Fig. 123

Colors and Stitches:

- • Eggshell Continental No. 1
- I Purple Continental No. 1
- / Rose Continental No. 1
- − Yellow Continental No. 1
- 1 Purple Basketweave No. 1
- 2 Rose Basketweave No. 1
- 3 Gold Diagonal Mosaic No. 1
- 4 Eggshell Basketweave No. 1

Yarn Requirements:

Eggshell—20 yards
Purple—3½ yards
Rose—4½ yards
Yellow—1 yard
Gold—8 yards

Leo—July 23 through August 22

(6″ by 6″. Fig. 124 and Plate 100)

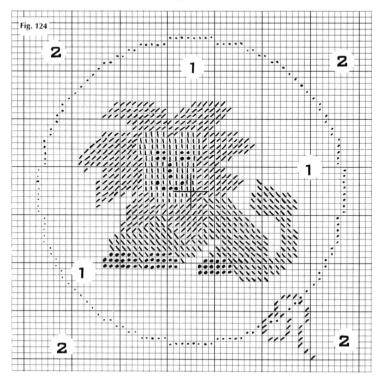

Fig. 124

Colors and Stitches:

- • Eggshell Continental No. 1
- / Dark Gold Continental No. 1 and Basketweave No. 1
- ● Brown Continental No. 1
- I Yellow Continental No. 1
- \ Light Gold Basketweave No. 1
- 1 Eggshell Basketweave No. 1
- 2 Dark Blue Scotch No. 1 and Scotch No. 2 Alternating

Yarn Requirements:

Eggshell—21 yards
Dark Gold—3½ yards
Brown—1 yard
Yellow—1 yard
Light Gold—3 yards
Dark Blue—8 yards

Plate 100. The Zodiac Designs are Taurus (upper left), Gemini (lower left), Cancer (upper right) and Leo (lower right). They have been made into pincushions, tote bag appliqués, wall hangings, and pencil cups.

Virgo—August 23 through September 22
(6″ by 6″. Fig. 125 and Plate 101)

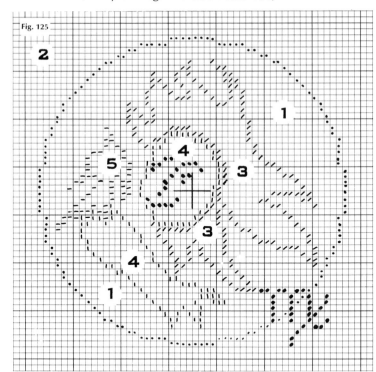

Colors and Stitches:

- • Eggshell Continental No. 1
- / Gold Continental No. 1
- I Pink Continental No. 1
- – Green Continental No. 1
- • Black Continental No. 1
- 1 Eggshell Basketweave No. 1
- 2 Blue Diagonal Mosaic No. 2
- 3 Gold Basketweave No. 1
- 4 Pink Basketweave No. 1
- 5 Green Basketweave No. 1

Yarn Requirements:

Eggshell—21 yards
Gold—4 yards
Pink—4 yards
Green—1 yard
Black—1 yard
Blue—7 yards

Libra—September 23 through October 22
(6″ by 6″. Fig. 126 and Plate 101)

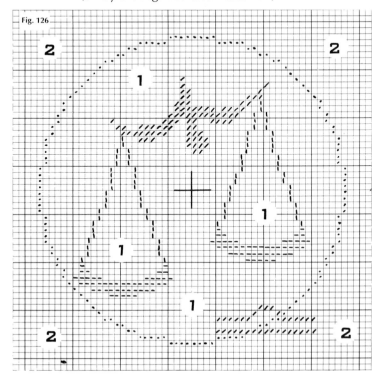

Colors and Stitches:

- • Eggshell Continental No. 1
- / Gold Continental No. 1
- I Yellow Continental No. 1
- – Dark Blue Continental No. 1
- 1 Eggshell Basketweave No. 1
- 2 Light Blue Mosaic No. 1

Yarn Requirements:

Eggshell—21 yards
Gold—2 yards
Yellow—2 yards
Dark Blue—2 yards
Light Blue—9 yards

Scorpio—October 23 through November 21
(6″ by 6″. Fig. 127 and Plate 101)

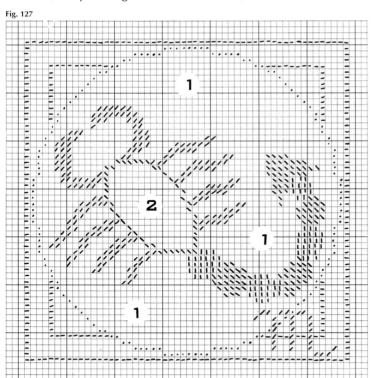

Fig. 127

Colors and Stitches:

- Eggshell Continental No. 1
- / Black Continental No. 1
- \ Dark Rust Continental No. 1
- I Light Rust Continental No. 1
- − Brown Continental No. 2
- 1 Eggshell Basketweave No. 1
- 2 Dark Rust Basketweave No. 1
  Outside Borders Dark Rust Scotch No. 2 between the rows of Brown Continental No. 2

Yarn Requirements:

Eggshell—20 yards
Black—4 yards
Dark Rust—8 yards
Light Rust—2 yards
Brown—4 yards

Sagittarius—November 22 through December 21
(6″ by 6″. Fig. 128 and Plate 101)

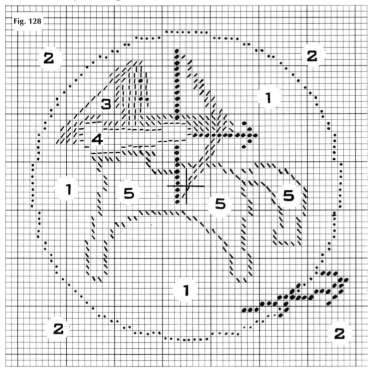

Fig. 128

Colors and Stitches:

- Eggshell Continental No. 1
- ● Black Continental No. 1
- / Gold Continental No. 1
- − Light Blue Continental No. 1
- \ Dark Blue Continental No. 1
- I Pink Continental No. 1
- 1 Eggshell Continental No. 1
- 2 Dark Blue Scotch No. 3 and Scotch No. 4 Alternating
- 3 Gold Basketweave No. 1
- 4 Light Blue Basketweave No. 1
- 5 Dark Blue Basketweave No. 1

Yarn Requirements:

Eggshell—20 yards
Black—1 yard
Gold—1½ yards
Light Blue—4 yards
Dark Blue—9 yards
Pink—¾ yard

177

Plate 101. The Zodiac Designs are Virgo (lower left), *Libra* (upper right) *Scorpio* (upper left) *and Sagittarius* (lower right). *They have been made into sachets, pillow appliqués, wall hangings, and notebook appliqués.*

Chapter 3

Stitches

This chapter contains 47 of the basic and more decorative needlepoint stitches. The graph lines represent the threads of the canvas. In each case the needle comes up through the canvas in the hole numbered 1 and goes back down through the canvas in the hole numbered 2. The needle comes up through each succeeding odd number and goes down through the canvas at each succeeding even number. The first row of stitches is drawn in the heavier line and the second row of stitches is drawn in the thinner line. If the numbers are upside down for the second row, this means that the canvas is turned upside down for the second row.

Continental No. 1

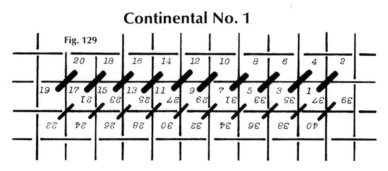

Fig. 129

Continental No. 2

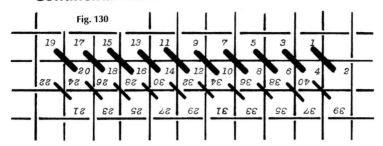

Fig. 130

Basketweave No. 1

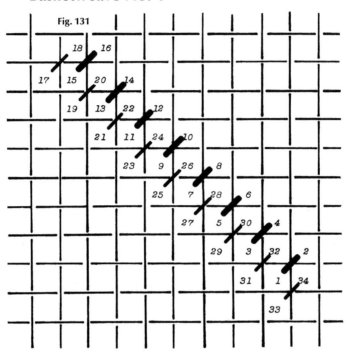

Fig. 131

Basketweave No. 2

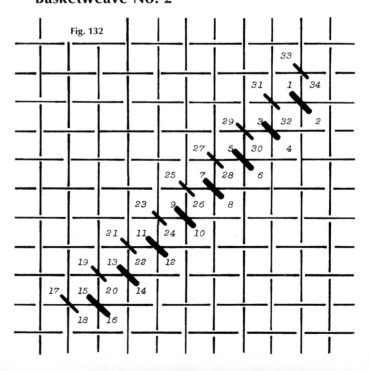

Fig. 132

Tied

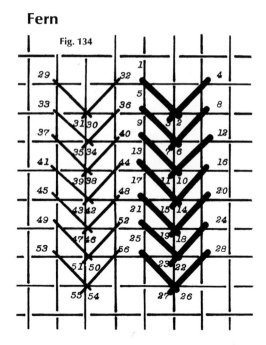

Fig. 133

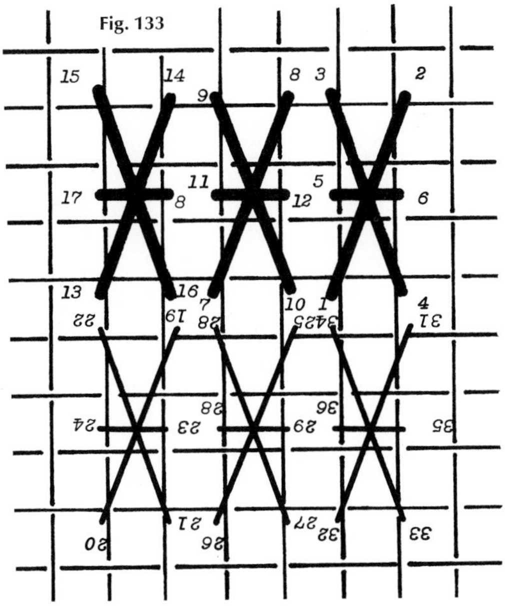

Fern

Fig. 134

Straight Cross

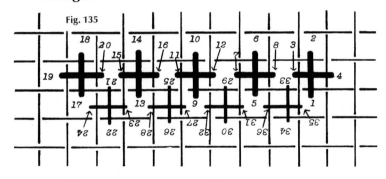

Fig. 135

Cashmere No. 1

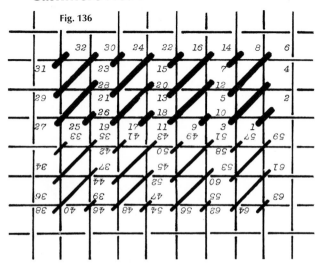

Fig. 136

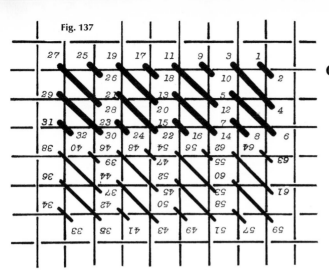

Cashmere No. 2

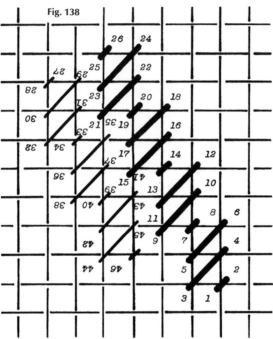

Diagonal Cashmere

Byzantine

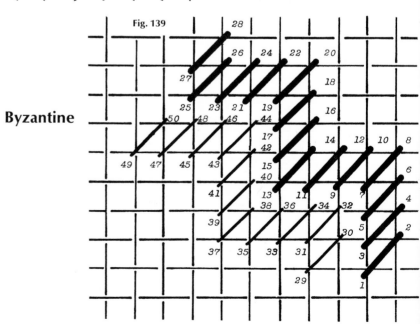

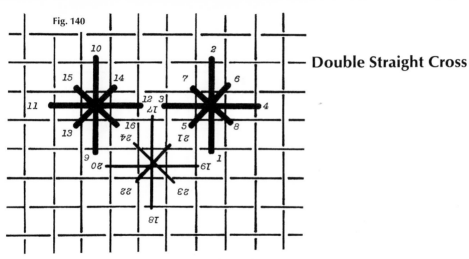

Double Straight Cross

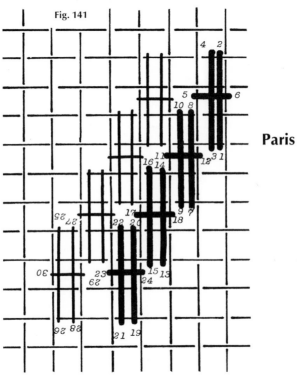

Paris

Web

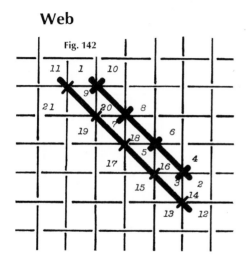

Smyrna

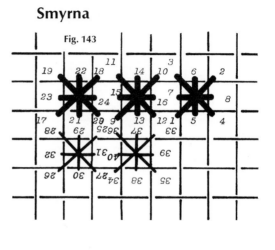

Stem No. 1

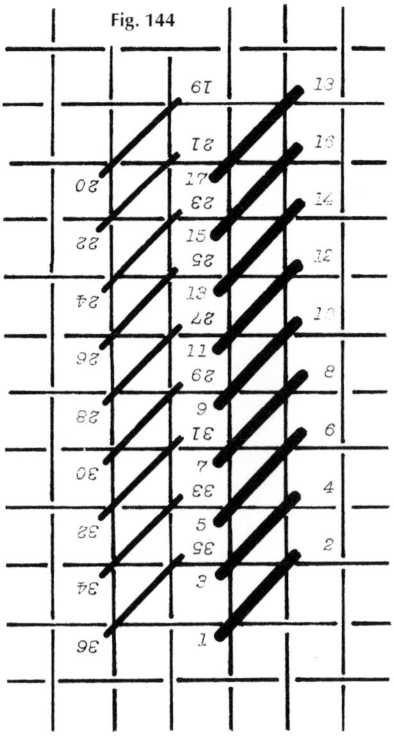

Fig. 144

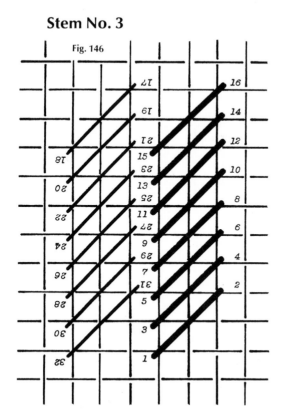

Stem No. 2

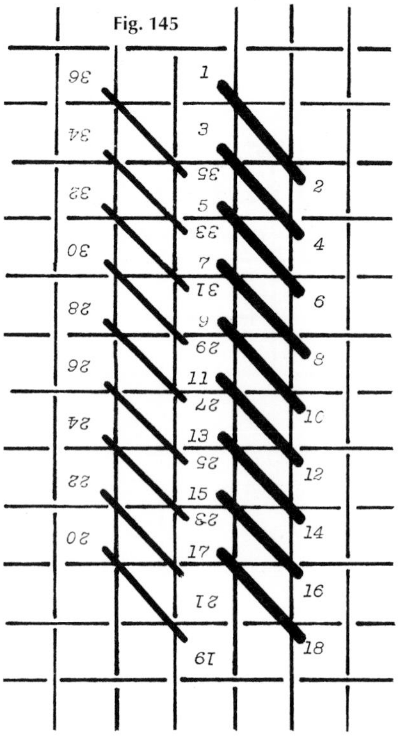

Fig. 145

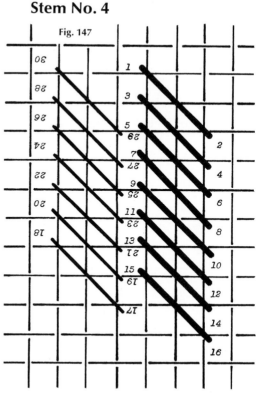

Stem No. 3

Fig. 146

Stem No. 4

Fig. 147

Stem No. 5

Fig. 148

Knitting

Fig. 149

Scotch No. 1

Fig. 150

Scotch No. 2

Fig. 151

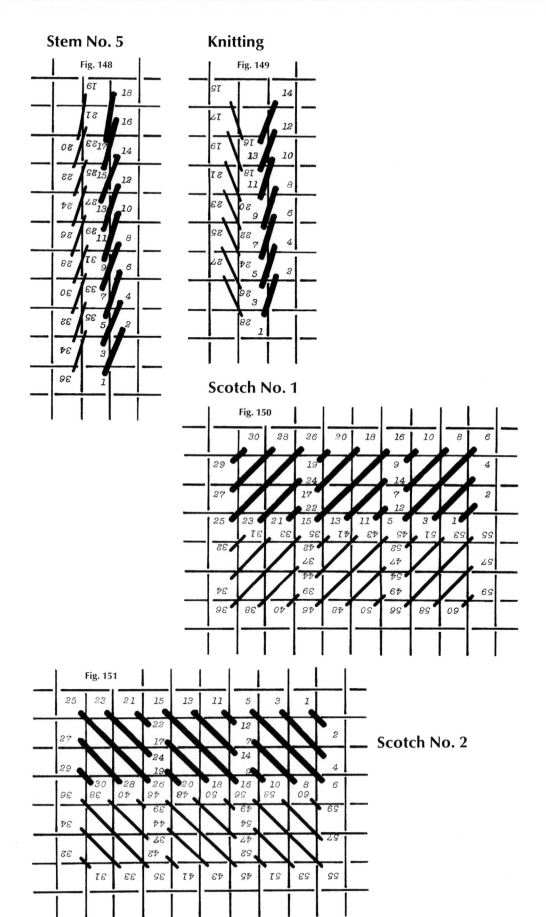

185

Scotch No. 3

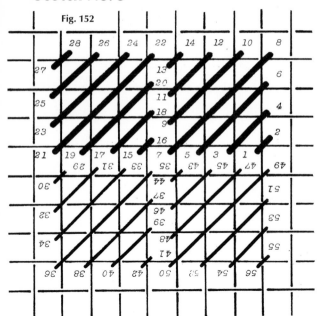

Fig. 152

Scotch No. 4

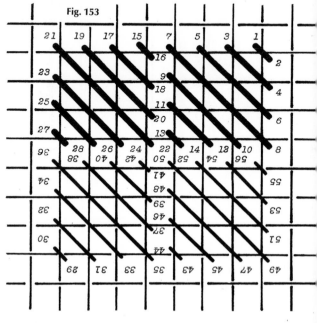

Fig. 153

Leaf

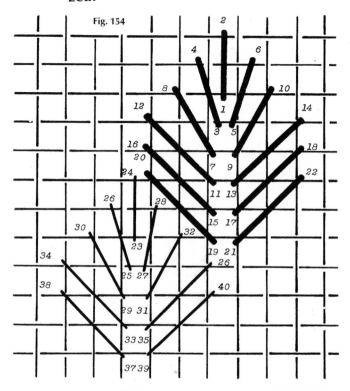

Fig. 154

186

Large and Upright Cross

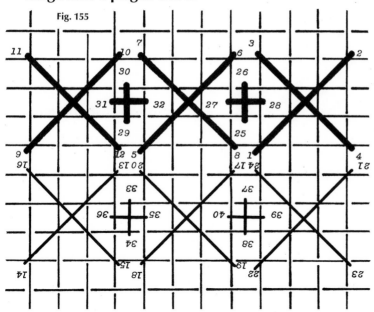

Fig. 155

Straight Gobelin

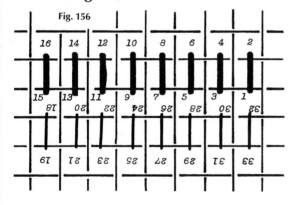

Fig. 156

Interlocking Gobelin

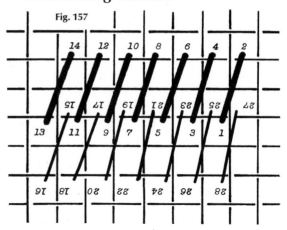

Fig. 157

Slanting Gobelin No. 1

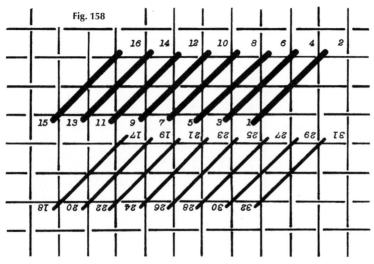

Fig. 158

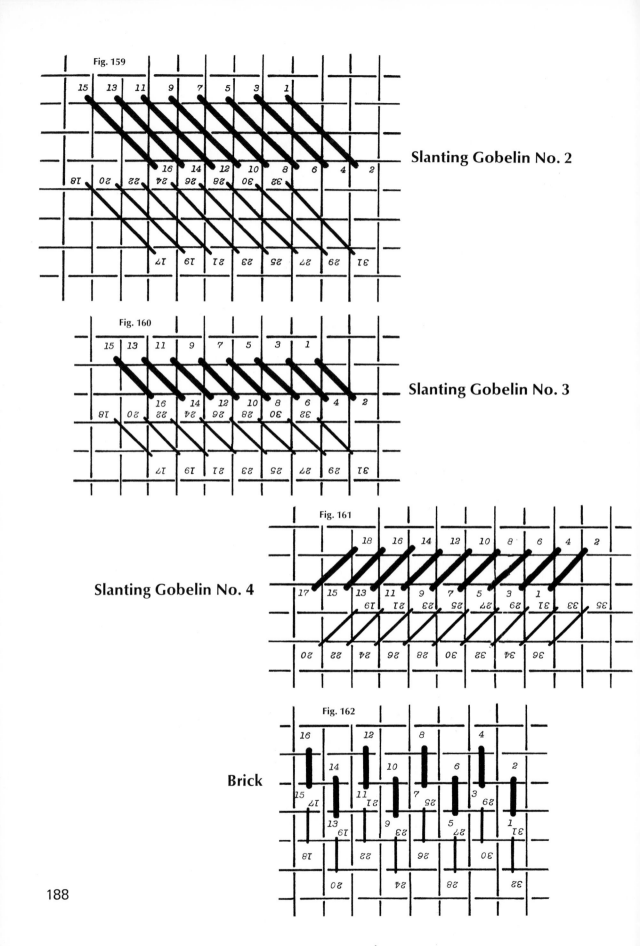

Fig. 159

Slanting Gobelin No. 2

Fig. 160

Slanting Gobelin No. 3

Slanting Gobelin No. 4

Fig. 161

Brick

Fig. 162

Knotted

Mosaic No. 1

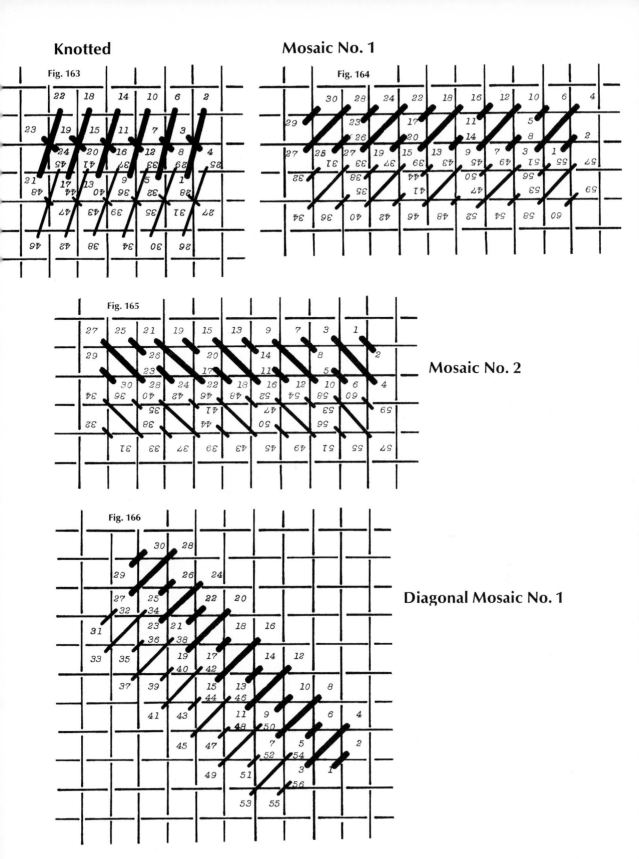

Fig. 163

Fig. 164

Fig. 165

Mosaic No. 2

Fig. 166

Diagonal Mosaic No. 1

Diagonal Mosaic No. 2

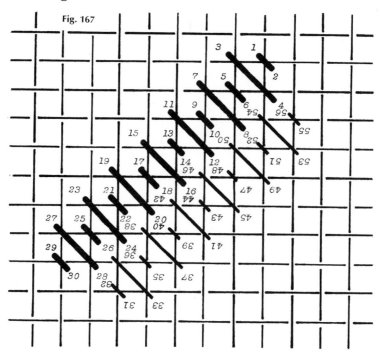

Fig. 167

Diagonal Mosaic No. 3

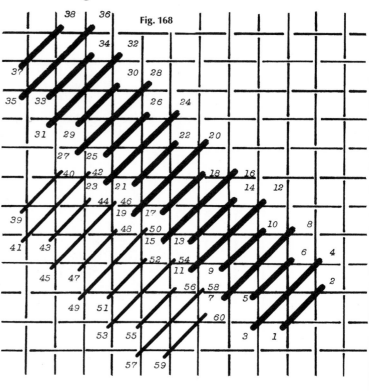

Fig. 168

Diagonal Mosaic No. 4

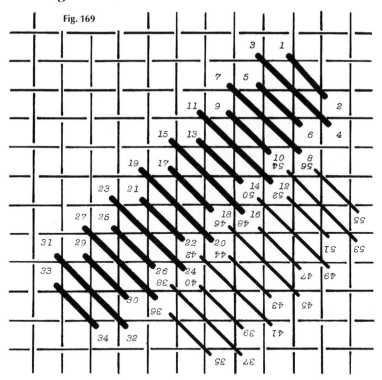

Fig. 169

French Knot

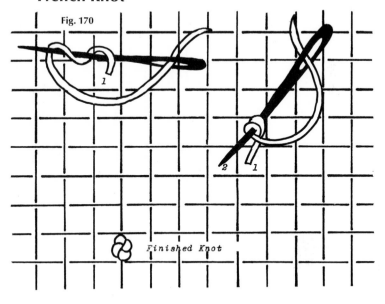

Fig. 170

Finished Knot

Milanese

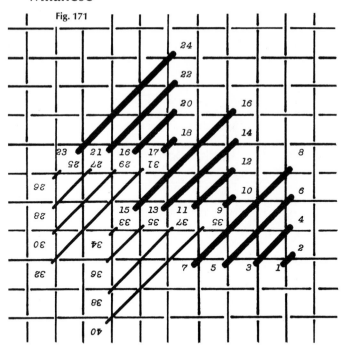

Fig. 171

Vertical Satin

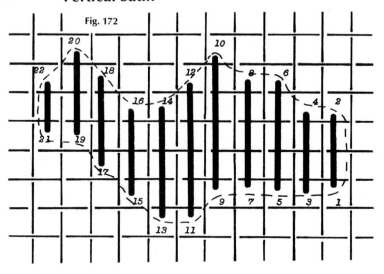

Fig. 172

192

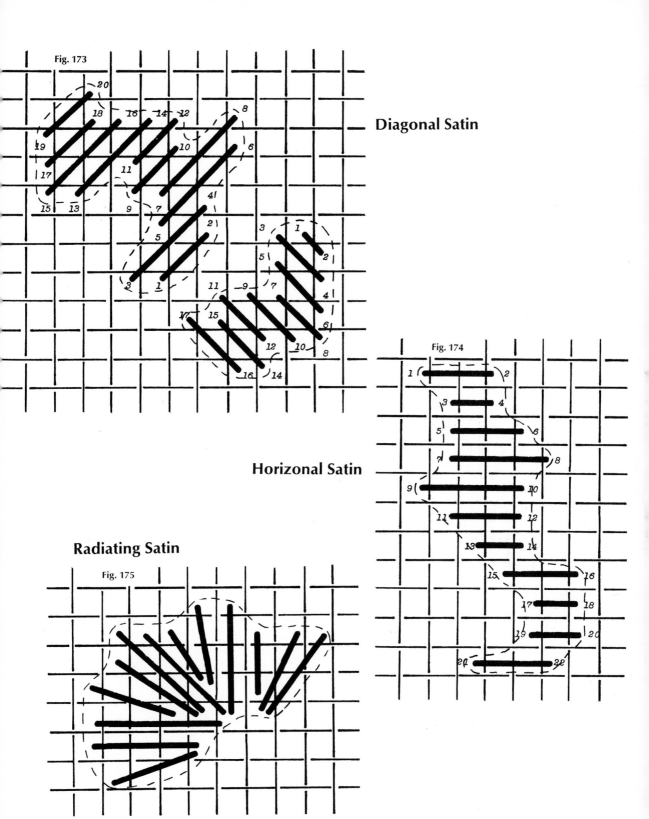

Diagonal Satin

Horizonal Satin

Radiating Satin

193

Chapter 4

Finishing Projects

BLOCKING

During needlepointing, certain stitches pull the canvas out of shape. Before the canvas can be made into the finished project, it must be blocked, or stretched back into its original shape, placing it face down on the board. The blocking board should be a clean, flat plywood or composition board, larger than the canvas. Cover the board with several layers of brown wrapping paper and draw the square outline of the canvas on the top paper. Tack or staple one side of the canvas to the corresponding side of the pattern. Drive the tacks, staples, or pushpins no more than ¾ of the way into the board and place them ½ to 1″ apart, close to the outside edge of the canvas. Pull the side of the canvas that slants toward the center of the board back to the pattern boundary, and tack or staple it as close to the line as possible. Pull the two remaining sides as close to their respective pattern boundaries as possible and tack or staple into place. Dampen the back of the needlepoint, but do not saturate it. Leave the canvas on the blocking board in a cool, dry place until completely dry. Remove each tack, staple, or pushpin individually. If you were unable to stretch the canvas to its original shape the first time, repeat the process as many times as necessary. As soon after blocking as possible, mount the needlepoint so that it retains its proper shape.

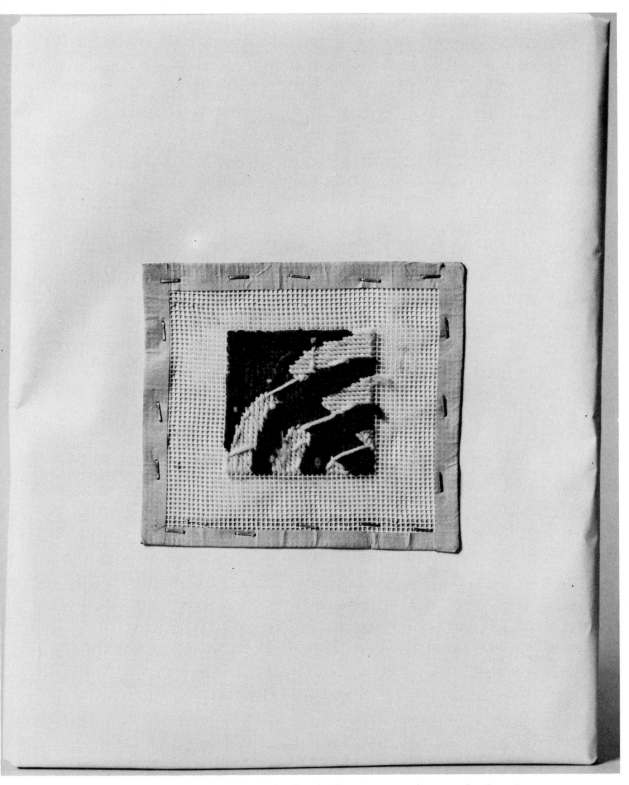

Plate 102. Blocking means stretching the finished canvas straight on a flat board to return it to its original square shape.

MOUNTING PROJECTS

In most cases, if you can successfully work needlepoint you can successfully mount your finished needlepoint. If you treat the finished canvas as you would a heavy piece of upholstery fabric, which in effect it is, many of the problems associated with finishing off needlepoint can be eliminated.

Knife-Edged Pillow

Knife-edged pillows are the simplest and quickest to make. Cut backing fabric 1" larger than the finished needlepoint. Pin and baste the two pieces together, right sides facing each other. Stitch together, leaving one side open. Turn right side out through the opening. Insert a pillow filler and stitch the opening closed.

Welting-Edged Pillow

Sew the welting on the face of the needlepoint about ⅛" from the outside edge. The raw edge of the welting must be toward the outside of the canvas. Cut backing fabric 1" larger than the finished needlepoint. Pin and baste the two pieces together, right sides facing each other. Stitch together on top of the row of stitches that you made when the welting was sewn onto the needlepoint, leaving one side open. Turn right side out through the opening. Insert a pillow filler and stitch the opening closed.

Appliquéd Pillows

Small pieces of needlepoint may be appliquéd to fabric, making them do the work of a much larger piece. Cut two pieces of fabric for the front and back of the pillow. Trim the canvas, leaving three to five rows of blank canvas on all sides. Apply a thin coat of upholstery glue to the raw edges of canvas. Pin and baste the needlepoint to the desired position on the front piece of fabric. Sew in place, leaving the canvas exposed. Pin and sew trim over the raw canvas and the outside row of finished needlepoint. Trim may be glued instead. Proceed with making the knife-edged or welting-edged pillow.

Framed Pictures

Cut a piece of ¼" plywood the same size as the finished needlepoint. Lay the plywood, smooth side down, on the back of the needlepoint. Tack or staple the center of each side to the back of the plywood. Check to make sure that the needlepoint is centered. Stretch the canvas tight and tack or staple every ½ to 1" on the back. When selecting a frame, make sure that it is deep enough to accommodate the thickness of the needlepoint, plywood, and glass, if used.

Trim-Edged Pictures

Cut a composition board, ½ or ¾" plywood backing board, ½" smaller than the finished background area of the needlepoint. Mount the needlepoint on the board as described above for Framed Pictures. Make sure that the background covers the front edge of the board and extends several rows down the edge of the board. Glue upholstery trim, moss fringe, or other trim around the outside edge of the board, making sure that all raw canvas is covered.

Double-Mounted Pictures

Mount the needlepoint as described above for a Trim-Edged Picture. Cut a second board several inches larger than the needlepoint-covered board and cover with fabric. Lay the fabric-covered board, *face up,* on the table. Lay the needlepoint-covered board, *face up,* in the center of the fabric-covered board. Glue the two boards together. For added security, screw the two boards together from the back.

Appliqué-Mounted Pictures

Cut a backing board of composition board, ½ or ¾″ plywood, the size desired for the picture, and cover with fabric. Trim the canvas, leaving three to five rows of blank canvas on all sides. Apply a thin coat of upholstery glue to the raw edges of the canvas. Place the needlepoint in the desired position on the face of the fabric-covered board and tack or staple in place. Glue upholstery trim, moss fringe, or other trim over the raw canvas and outside row of finished needlepoint.

Eyeglass Cases

Trim the canvas to within ⅜″ of the finished needlepoint. Turn the canvas margins to the back and baste in place. Place the two pieces of canvas together, wrong sides facing each other. Sew the two sides and bottom together. Sew trim, if desired, around the two sides and bottom. Tuck the ends of the trim inside the top of the case and stitch in place. To determine the size of the lining fabric, measure the length of the finished case. Double this measurement and add 1″. Measure the width of the finished case and add 1″. Cut lining fabric this size. Fold the fabric in half, crosswise, right sides facing each other. Sew the two sides together using a ½″ seam allowance. Fold down the top edges to the outside by ½″. Slip the lining inside the case and stitch to the top of the needlepoint.

Checkbook Covers

Follow the instructions for making an eyeglass case, with the following changes.
1. Leave one long side open instead of the top.
2. To determine the size of the lining fabric, measure the length of the finished case and add 1″. Measure the width of the finished case. Double this measurement and add 1″. Fold the lining fabric in half, lengthwise, with the right sides together.
3. Continue with the directions for the eyeglass case except that one long side is left open instead of the top.

Pincushions or Sachets

Follow the instructions for making pillows and fill with sachet mixture. Because of the thickness of the needlepoint, use a lightweight backing fabric. Also, pack the finished sachet in with some sachet mixture for a period of time so that the needlepoint will be permeated with the scent.

Belts

Trim the canvas to within ½″ of the finished needlepoint. Turn the canvas margins to the back and baste in place. Cut a strip of medium-weight, nonwoven interfacing ⅛" smaller than the finished needlepoint. With iron, press on the wrong side of the belt. Cut a 4" length of ribbon the same width as the finished needlepoint. Place a small eyelet in the center of the ribbon to accommodate the buckle prong. Fold the ribbon in half and place it on the shank of the buckle. Sew the ribbon and buckle to the back of the belt. Stitch a ribbon backing inside the belt. Using a eyelet setter or the services of a shoemaker, set eyelets at the opposite end.

Box Tops

The needlepoint should be ¾" larger than the box top. Trim the canvas to within three or four mesh of the finished canvas. Pad the top of the box with cotton, acrylic fiber, or other similar material. Tack or staple the needlepoint over the padded top, making sure that it is tight and straight. Glue upholstery trim over the raw canvas and tacks or staples.

Coasters

Trim the canvas to within three or four mesh of the finished canvas. Turn the canvas margins to the back and baste in place. Cut a piece of felt the same size as the finished needlepoint. Glue the felt to the back of the needlepoint. Do not use too much glue or it may come through the needlepoint. Place some weight on the coaster while it is drying.

Tassels

Fig. 176

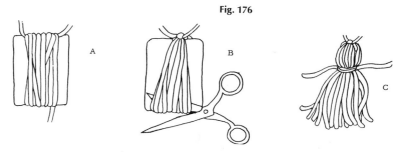

Cut a piece of cardboard as wide as you want the tassel to be long. Wrap several strands of yarn around the cardboard until the tassel is as fat as you want it to be. Thread a short piece of yarn under the wrapped yarn, at the top of the cardboard, and tie tightly. Cut the wrapped yarn at the bottom. Tie the tassel together a short distance from the top with a piece of yarn. Trim the bottom of the tassel and sew to the corner of the project.

CARE AND CLEANING OF FINISHED NEEDLEPOINT

Finished needlepoint should be treated like any good upholstery fabric. It is extremely strong, and if properly cared for will last a lifetime and beyond.

The newly finished and mounted project should be sprayed with Scotchgard or other similar fabric protector. Individual spots and strains should be removed with a high-quality spot remover. Do not brush the stitches with a stiff cleaning brush as it will tear loose yarn fibers and create an unpleasant uneven surface. If you find it necessary to brush, use a soft brush and always brush in the same direction that the stitches slant. When the time for cleaning comes, consult a reputable cleaner who is familiar with needlepoint. One bad cleaning can ruin a piece of needlepoint. Keep your needlepoint out of areas of extraordinary wear and, of course, to prevent fading, keep it out of direct sunlight. Beyond that, relax and enjoy your finished needlepoint.

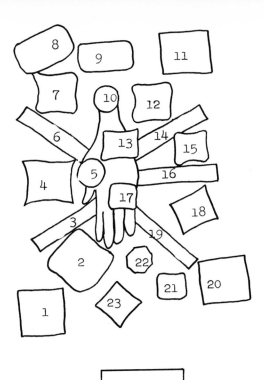

KEYED DIAGRAMS FOR COLOR SECTION

COLOR PLATE 1

1—Leo Zodiac
2—Pisces Zodiac
3—Hearts Sash
4—Gemini Zodiac
5—Tulip Coaster
6—Tulips Belt
7—Tulip Pincushion
8—Small Dog Eyeglass Case
9—Stars and Stripes Eyeglass Case
10—Mushroom Coaster
11—Cancer Zodiac
12—Union Jack Sachet
13—Rectangles Sachet
14—Sailboat Belt
15—Pierced Heart Pincushion
16—Ladybug Sash
17—Fleur-de-Lys Pincushion
18—Tick-Tack-Toe Pincushion
19—Folded Ribbon Belt
20—Aquarius Zodiac
21—Chart Sampler Pincushion
22—Rainbow Coaster
23—Diamond Pincushion

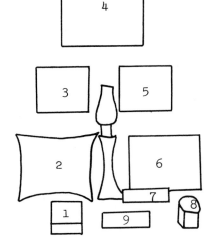

COLOR PLATE 2

1—Griffin Box Top
2—Hexagon Sampler Pillow
3—Comet 1906 Wall Hanging
4—Scallop Sunburst Wall Hanging
5—Keeton 1913 Wall Hanging
6—Lyre and Cross Box Top
7—Fleur-de-Lys and Cross Box Top
8—Napoleonic Bee Box Top
9—Scroll Leaf Box Top

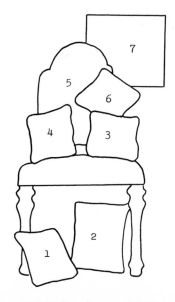

COLOR PLATE 3

1—Persian Fragment No. 1
2—Cube Graphic Pillow
3—Tiger Skin Pillow
4—Flambeaux Pillow
5—Fleur-de-Lys and Cross Chair Back
6—Pre-Columbian Medallion Pillow
7—Country Scene Wall Hanging

COLOR PLATE 4

1—Four Butterflies Pillow
2—Circle of Flowers Pillow
3—Four Flowers Pillow
4—Splash of Flowers Pillow
5—Swirl of Butterflies Pillow
6—Trellis of Roses Pillow
7—Wise Owl Pillow
8—Anemones Pillow

COLOR PLATE 5

1—Witty Owl Pillow
2—Three Carnations Pillow
3—Sunflower Pillow
4—Strawberries and Flowers Pillow
5—Pennsylvania Dutch Hearts Pillow
6—Impressionistic Flowers Pillow
7—Five Mushrooms Pillow

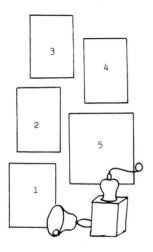

COLOR PLATE 6

1—Little Miss Muffet Wall Hanging
2—Hickory Dickory Dock Wall Hanging
3—Jack and Jill Wall Hanging
4—Humpty Dumpty Wall Hanging
5—Jonah in the Whale Wall Hanging

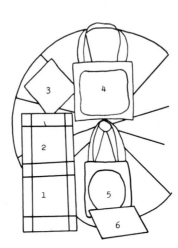

COLOR PLATE 7

1—Tulip Flower Wall Hanging
2—Small Flower Wall Hanging
3—Persian Fragment No. 2
4—Clown Face Tote Bag
5—Fat Mushroom Tote Bag
6—Ladybug on Leaves Wall Hanging

COLOR PLATE 8

1—Sliced Mushroom Wall Hanging
2—Basket of Cherries Wall Hanging
3—Sliced Avocado Wall Hanging
4—Still Life Wall Hanging
5—Sliced Lemon Wall Hanging
6—Sliced Apple Wall Hanging
7—Basket of Strawberries Wall Hanging

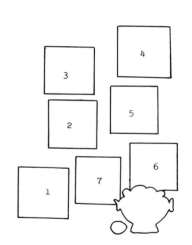

Suppliers

American Handicrafts, 510 Sixth Avenue, New York, N.Y., 10014

Barnes & Blake, Ltd., G.P.O. Box 2387, New York, N.Y., 10001 or at The Stitching Post, Brentano's, 586 Fifth Avenue, New York, N.Y., 10036

Emile Bernat & Sons, 230 Fifth Avenue, New York, N.Y., 10001

Boutique Margot, 26 West 54th Street, New York, N.Y., 10019

Coats & Clark, 430 Park Avenue, New York, N.Y., 10022

Columbia-Minerva Corp., 295 Fifth Avenue, New York, N.Y., 10010

D.M.C. Corp., 107 Trumbull Street, Elizabeth, N.J., 07206

Dritz, Scovill Mfg. Corp., 350 Fifth Avenue, New York, N.Y., 10001

Fibre Yarn, 840 Sixth Avenue, New York, N.Y., 10001

Minuet, 275 Seventh Avenue, New York, N.Y., 10001

Paternayan Brothers, 312 East 95th Street, New York, N.Y., 10028

The Stitchery, Wellesley, Mass., 02181

Joan Toggitt, Ltd., 1170 Broadway, Room 406, New York, N.Y., 10001

Bernhard Ulmann Co., 30-20 Thomson Avenue, Long Island City, N.Y., 11101

Woolcraft, Ltd., Alice Godkin, #4 Trading Company Building, Regina, Sask., Canada

Index